Hold Fast to God

Wisdom from The Early Church

Jeanne Kun, Editor

the**WORD**
among us

The Word Among Us Press
9639 Doctor Perry Road
Ijamsville, Maryland   21754
ISBN: 0-932085-57-1

www.wau.org

The English translation of the sermons of the Fathers from
The Liturgy of the Hours © 1974, International Committee on
English in the Liturgy, Inc. All rights reserved.

Wisdom Series Editor: Patricia Mitchell
Cover Design by Christopher Ranck

Made and printed in the United States of America

Library of Congress Cataloging-in-Publication Data

Hold fast to god: wisdom from the early church / Jeanne Kun, editor.
     p.cm includes index.
ISBN 0-932085-57-1
   1. Christian Life. 2. Christian Literature, Early. I. Kun, Jeanne, 1951-

BR63 .H65 2001   2001026787
270.1–dc21

Table of Contents

Introduction

Basil ... Augustine ... Irenaeus ... Chrysostom
... Ambrose ... Christianity's ancient churchmen
form a litany of names vaguely familiar to us, names
we speak with respect or perhaps even with reverence.
Many of us, however, don't know all that much
about the people to whom these names belong, and
still less about what they thought and taught. We're
familiar with the apostles and evangelists who wrote
the New Testament and laid the foundations of the
church—well-known names like Matthew and John,
Peter and Paul. But they were soon followed by many
more believers who contributed to the explosion of
Christianity beyond Jerusalem and Rome. And among
these were the people we now call the Fathers of the
Church.

The first of the "Fathers" were born while some of
the apostles were still alive. They lived and worked in
the invigorating and turbulent atmosphere of the

primitive church. In the second and third centuries A.D., a new generation arose which guided the young church through times of growth and persecution. In the fourth century and beyond, various Fathers engaged in heated (and often politically charged) controversies concerning issues of faith, doctrine, and theology as the church began to clarify and refine its teaching.

Thus, the Fathers span the formative years of Christianity and its spread throughout the Roman Empire and the Mediterranean world, from the latter half of the first century to the mid-eighth century and later. Their spirit and influence continued well into the Middle Ages in the Western church, where St. Bernard of Clairvaux (1090-1153) has been called the "last of the Fathers." In the Eastern church, it is often said that the patristic spirit never really disappeared.

Shapers of the Church

Reading the works of the Fathers gives us an opportunity to see how the church took shape and was guided by people who were passionate in their love for Jesus. In the fourth century, for instance, the bishop Athanasius was so moved by the redemption he had received in Christ that he wrote his classic *On the Incarnation*. This famous treatise describes how Jesus took real human flesh from Mary so that he could redeem our fallen nature and restore us all to the image of God. Another early bishop, Ambrose of Milan, brought the prayers of ancient Israel alive for Christian believers in his *Explanations of the Psalms*.

Whether preaching about prayer, expounding on God's mercy, or meeting the challenges of the gospel, the Fathers were as concerned for the people in their churches as priests and bishops are today. They didn't just speak about abstract theories. They taught their brothers and sisters how to put their faith into action and draw unbelievers into the life that had transformed them. They were called upon frequently to defend the gospel against heresies and distortions of the truth, and in the process forged beautiful and brilliant statements that have guided the church for centuries. With an unshakable faith in Jesus, many of them also suffered greatly for their willingness to uphold the gospel—whether through persecution, exile, or even martyrdom.

A Vast Chorus

While the Fathers of the Church share a great unity in the faith, their writings reflect a wide diversity of culture, language, and experience. We meet among them Romans, Africans, Syrians, Greeks, and Europeans. Each man's work is stamped by his own personality and experience, and yet together they form a vast chorus whose voices blend in rich harmony as they proclaim Jesus Christ and the gospel of salvation.

Because the sermons and teachings of the Fathers were written centuries ago, they reflect some unfamiliar literary styles. Poetic images, colorful allegories, and rich symbolism abound, often where we might expect nothing more than logical explanation. Yet their insights into the word of God and the mysteries of Christ can open up for us endless horizons of faith.

The voices of the early church Fathers sing of the beauty, promise, and challenge held out to us in the gospel. They resound with a passionate love for God and his ways, and awaken that same love in us. With a freshness and vitality that has lasted for centuries, their words remind us of the inheritance that is ours in Christ. As you listen to their voices and explore their writings, these ancient churchmen can become much more to you than revered names. May you find in the Fathers true companions in faith to accompany you on the way to God's kingdom.

Jeanne Kun
Editor

1

Grace and Mercy

ALL MY HOPE
LIES IN YOUR GREAT MERCY

Saint Augustine, Bishop

[*From the Confessions*]

Where did I find you, that I came to know you? You were not within my memory before I learned of you. Where, then, did I find you before I came to know you, if not within yourself, far above me? We come to you and go from you, but no place is involved in this process. In every place, O Truth, you are present to those who seek your help, and at one and the same time you answer all, though they seek your counsel on different matters.

You respond clearly, but not everyone hears clearly. All ask what they wish, but do not always hear the answer they wish. Your best servant is he who is intent not so much on hearing his petition answered, as rather on willing whatever he hears from you.

Late have I loved you, O Beauty ever ancient, ever new, late have I loved you! You were within me, but I was outside, and it was there that I searched for you. In my unloveliness I plunged into the lovely things which you created. You were with me, but I was not with you. Created things kept me from you; yet if they had not been in you they would not have been at all. You called, you shouted, and you broke through my deafness. You flashed, you shone, and you dispelled my blindness. You breathed your fragrance on me; I drew in breath and now I pant for you. I have tasted you; now I hunger and thirst for more. You touched me, and I burned for your peace.

When once I shall be united to you with my whole being, I shall at last be free of sorrow and toil. Then my life will be alive, filled entirely with you. When you fill someone, you relieve him of his burden, but because I am not yet filled with you, I am a burden to myself. My joy when I should be weeping struggles with my sorrows when I should be rejoicing. I know not where victory lies. Woe is me! Lord, have mercy on me! My evil sorrows and good joys are at war with one another. I know not where victory lies. Woe is me! Lord, have mercy! Woe is me! I make no effort to conceal my wounds. You are my physician, I your patient. You are merciful; I stand in need of mercy.

Is not the life of man upon earth a trial? Who would want troubles and difficulties? You command us to endure them, not to love them. No person loves what he endures, though he may love the act of enduring. For even if he is happy to endure his own burden, he would still prefer that the burden not exist. I long for prosperity in times of adversity, and I fear adversity when times are good. Yet what middle ground is there between these two extremes where the life of man would be other than trial? Pity the prosperity of this world, pity it once and again, for it corrupts joy and brings the fear of adversity. Pity the adversity of this world, pity it again, then a third time; for it fills men with a longing for prosperity, and because adversity itself is hard for them to bear and can even break their endurance. *Is not the life of man upon earth a trial,* a continuous trial?

All my hope lies only in your great mercy. ❧

WHERE SIN ABOUNDED
GRACE HAS OVERFLOWED

Saint Bernard, Abbot

[*From a Sermon on the Song of Songs*]

Where can the weak find a place of firm security and peace, except in the wounds of the Savior? Indeed, the more secure is my place there the more he can do to help me. The world rages, the flesh is heavy, and the devil lays his snares, but I do not fall, for my feet are planted on firm rock. I may have sinned gravely. My conscience would be distressed, but it would not be in turmoil, for I would recall the wounds of the Lord: *he was wounded for our iniquities*. What sin is there so deadly that it cannot be pardoned by the death of Christ? And so if I bear in mind this strong, effective remedy, I can never again be terrified by the malignancy of sin.

Surely the man who said: *My sin is too great to merit pardon*, was wrong. He was speaking as though he were not a member of Christ and had no share in his merits, so that he could claim them as his own, as a member of the body can claim what belongs to the head. As for me, what can I appropriate that I lack from the heart of the Lord who abounds in mercy? They pierced his hands and feet and opened his side with a spear. Through the openings of these wounds I may drink *honey from the rock and oil from the hardest stone*: that is, I may *taste and see that the Lord is sweet*.

He was thinking thoughts of peace, and I did not know it, *for who knows the mind of the Lord, or who has been his counselor?* But the piercing nail has become a key to unlock the door, that I may see the good will of the Lord. And what can I see as I look through the hole? Both the nail and the wound cry out that God was in Christ reconciling the world to himself. *The sword pierced his soul and came close to his heart*, so that he might be able to feel compassion for me in my weaknesses.

Through these sacred wounds we can see the secret of his heart, the great mystery of love, *the sincerity of his mercy with which he visited us from on high*. Where have your love, your mercy, your compassion shone out more luminously than in your wounds, sweet, gentle Lord of mercy? More mercy than this no one has than that he lay down his life for those who are doomed to death.

My merit comes from his mercy; for I do not lack merit so long as he does not lack pity. And if the Lord's mercies are many, then I am rich in merits. For even if I am aware of many sins, what does it matter? *Where sin abounded grace has overflowed.* And if *the Lord's mercies are from all ages for ever,* I too *will sing of the mercies of the Lord for ever.* Will I not sing of my own righteousness? No, *Lord, I shall be mindful only of your justice.* Yet that too is my own; for God had made you my righteousness. ∾

IN THE FULLNESS OF TIME THE FULLNESS OF DIVINITY APPEARED

Saint Bernard, Abbot

[*From a Sermon*]

The *goodness and humanity of God our Savior have appeared in our midst.* We thank God for the many consolations he has given us during this sad exile of our pilgrimage here on earth. Before the Son of God became man his goodness was hidden, for God's mercy is eternal, but how could such goodness be recognized? It was promised, but it was not experienced, and as a result few believed in it. *Often and in many ways the Lord used to speak through the prophets.* Among other things, God said: *I think thoughts of peace and not of affliction.* But what did men respond, thinking thoughts of affliction and knowing nothing of peace? They said: *Peace, peace, there is no peace.* This response made the *angels of peace weep bitterly,* saying: *Lord, who has believed our message?* But now men believe because they see with their own eyes, and because *God's testimony has now become even more credible.* He has gone so far as to *pitch his tent in the sun* so even the dimmest eyes see him.

Notice that peace is not promised but sent to us; it is no longer deferred, it is given; peace is not prophesied but achieved. It is as if God the Father sent upon the earth a purse full of his mercy. This purse was burst open during the Lord's passion to pour forth its hidden contents—the price of our redemption. It was only a small purse, but it was very full. As the Scriptures tell us: *A little child has been given to us, but in him dwells all the fullness of the divine nature.* The fullness of time brought with it the fullness of divinity. God's Son came in the flesh so that mortal men could see and recognize God's kindness. When God reveals his humanity, his goodness cannot possibly remain hidden. To show his kindness what more could he do beyond taking my human form? My humanity, I say, not Adam's—that is, not such as he had before his fall.

How could he have shown his mercy more clearly than by taking on himself our condition? For our sake the Word of God became as grass. What better proof could he have given of his love? Scripture says: *Lord, what is man that you are mindful of him; why does your heart go out to him?* The incarnation teaches us how much God cares for us and what he thinks and feels about us. We should stop thinking of our own sufferings and remember what he has suffered. Let us think of all the Lord has done for us, and then we shall realize how his goodness appears through his humanity. The lesser he became through his human nature the greater was his goodness; the more he lowered himself for me, the dearer he is to me. *The goodness and humanity of God our Savior have appeared*, says the Apostle.

Truly great and manifest are the goodness and humanity of God. He has given us a most wonderful proof of his goodness by adding humanity to his own divine nature. ❧

TRUTH HAS ARISEN FROM THE EARTH, AND JUSTICE LOOKED DOWN FROM HEAVEN

Saint Augustine, Bishop

[*From a Sermon*]

Awake, mankind! For your sake God has become man. *Awake, you who sleep, rise up from the dead, and Christ will enlighten you.* I tell you again: for your sake, God became man.

You would have suffered eternal death, had he not been born in time. Never would you have been freed from sinful flesh, had he not taken on himself the likeness of sinful flesh. You would have suffered everlasting unhappiness, had it not been for this mercy. You would never have returned to life, had he not shared your death. You would have been lost if he had not hastened to your aid. You would have perished, had he not come.

Let us then joyfully celebrate the coming of our salvation and redemption. Let us celebrate the festive day on which he who is the great and eternal day came from the great and endless day of eternity into our own short day of time.

He has become our justice, our sanctification, our redemption, so that, as it is written: Let him who glories glory in the Lord.

Truth, then, has arisen from the earth: Christ who said, *I am the Truth,* was born of a virgin. *And justice looked down from heaven:* because believing in this new-born child, man is justified not by himself but by God.

Truth has arisen from the earth: because *the Word was made flesh. And justice looked down from heaven:* because *every good gift and every perfect gift is from above.*

Truth has arisen from the earth: flesh from Mary. *And justice looked down from heaven:* for man can receive nothing unless it has been given him from heaven.

Justified by faith, let us be at peace with God: for justice and peace have embraced one another. Through our Lord Jesus Christ: for Truth has arisen from the earth. Through whom we have access to that grace in which we stand, and our boast is in our hope of God's glory. He does not say: "of our glory," but *of God's glory: for justice* has not proceeded from us but has *looked down from heaven*. Therefore *he who glories, let him glory*, not in himself, but *in the Lord.*

For this reason, when our Lord was born of the Virgin, the message of the angelic voices was: *Glory to God in the highest, and peace to his people on earth.*

For how could there be peace on earth unless *Truth has arisen from the earth,* that is, unless Christ were born of our flesh? And *he is our peace who made the two into one:* that we might be men of good will, sweetly linked by the bond of unity.

Let us then rejoice in this grace, so that our glorying may bear witness to our good conscience by which we glory, not in ourselves, but in the Lord. That is why Scripture says: *He is my glory, the one who lifts up my head.* For what greater grace could God have made to dawn on us than to make his only Son become the son of man, so that a son of man might in his turn become son of God?

Ask if this were merited; ask for its reason, for its justification, and see whether you will find any other answer but sheer grace. ⟳

CHRIST DIED FOR ALL

Saint Augustine, Bishop

[*From the Confessions*]

The true Mediator was he whom you revealed to humble men in your secret mercy, and whom you sent so they might learn that same humility by following his example. This was the *Mediator between God and man, the man Christ Jesus,* who intervened between sinful mortals and the immortal Just One, himself mortal like men, and like God, just. Thus, since life and peace are the compensation for righteousness, he could, by a justice united with God, annul the death of sinners now justified, since he willed to share death with them.

Good Father, how you loved us, *sparing not your only Son but delivering him up for us sinners!* How you loved us, for whose sake he, *thinking it no robbery to be equal with you, was made subject to death on the cross.* He alone, free among the dead, *had the power to lay down his life and the power to take it up again.* For our sake he became in your sight both victor and victim—victor, indeed, because he was victim. For our sake, too, he became before you both priest and sacrifice—priest, indeed, because he was a sacrifice, changing us from slaves to sons by being your Son and serving us.

Rightly then have I firm hope that you will heal all my infirmities through him who sits at your right hand and *intercedes for us*. Otherwise I should despair. For great and numerous are these infirmities of mine, great indeed and numerous, but your medicine is mightier. We might have thought your Word remote from any union with man, and so have despaired of ourselves, if he had not *become flesh and dwelt among us*.

Crushed by my sins and the weight of my misery, I had taken thought in my heart and contemplated flight into the desert. But you stopped me and gave me comfort with the words: *Christ died for all, that those who live might no longer live for themselves but for him who died for them*.

Behold, Lord, I cast upon you my concern that I may live and *I shall meditate on the wonders of your law*. You know my ignorance and my weakness; teach me and heal me. Your only Son, in whom *are hidden all the treasures of wisdom and knowledge*, redeemed me with his blood. *Let not arrogant men speak evil of me.* For I meditate on my ransom, and I eat it and drink it and try to share it with others; though poor I want to be filled with it in the company of those who eat and are filled; and *they shall praise the Lord who seek him.* ༄

THE MYSTERY OF MAN'S RECONCILIATION WITH GOD

Saint Leo the Great, Pope

[*From a Letter*]

Lowliness is assured by majesty, weakness by power, mortality by eternity. To pay the debt of our sinful state, a nature that is incapable of suffering was joined to one that could suffer. Thus, in keeping with the healing that we needed, one and the same mediator between God and men, the man Jesus Christ, was able to die in one nature, and unable to die in the other.

He who is true God was therefore born in the complete and perfect nature of a true man, whole in his own nature, whole in ours. By our nature we mean what the Creator had fashioned in us from the beginning, and took to himself in order to restore it.

For in the Savior there was no trace of what the deceiver introduced and man, being misled, allowed to enter. It does not follow that because he submitted to sharing in our human weakness he therefore shared in our sins.

He took the nature of a servant without stain of sin, enlarging our humanity without diminishing his divinity. He emptied himself; though invisible he made himself visible, though Creator and Lord of all things he chose to be one of us mortal men. Yet this was the condescension of compassion, not the loss of omnipotence. So he who in the nature of God had created man, became in the nature of a servant, man himself.

Thus the Son of God enters this lowly world. He comes down from the throne of heaven, yet does not separate himself from the Father's glory. He is born in a new condition, by a new birth.

He was born in a new condition, for, invisible in his own nature, he became visible in ours. Beyond our grasp, he chose to come within our grasp. Existing before time began, he began to exist at a moment in time. Lord of the universe, he hid his infinite glory and took the nature of a servant. Incapable of suffering as God, he did not refuse to be a man, capable of suffering. Immortal, he chose to be subject to the laws of death.

He who is true God is also true man. There is no falsehood in this unity as long as the lowliness of man and the preeminence of God coexist in mutual relationship.

As God does not change by his condescension, so man is not swallowed up by being exalted. Each nature exercises its own activity, in communion with the other. The Word does what is proper to the Word, the flesh fulfills what is proper to the flesh.

One nature is resplendent with miracles, the other falls victim to injuries. As the Word does not lose equality with the Father's glory, so the flesh does not leave behind the nature of our race.

One and the same person—this must be said over and over again—is truly the Son of God and truly the son of man. He is God in virtue of the fact that *in the beginning was the Word, and the Word was with God, and the Word was God.* He is man in virtue of the fact that *the Word was made flesh, and dwelt among us.* ❧

IN CHRIST ARE THE FIRSTFRUITS OF THE RESURRECTION

Saint Irenaeus, Bishop

[*From a Treatise "Against Heresies"*]

The Word of God became man, the Son of God became the Son of Man, in order to unite man with himself and make him, by adoption, a son of God. Only by being united to one who is himself immune could we be preserved from corruption and death, and how else could this union have been achieved if he had not first become what we are? How else could what is corruptible and mortal in us have been swallowed up in his incorruptibility and immortality, to enable us to receive adoptive sonship? Therefore, the Son of God, our Lord, the Word of the Father, is also the son of man; he became the son of man by a human birth from Mary, a member of the human race.

The Lord himself has given us a sign here below and in the heights of heaven, a sign that man did not ask for because he never dreamt that such a thing would be possible. A virgin was with a child and she bore a son who is called Emmanuel, which means "God with us." He came down to the earth here below in search of the sheep that was lost, the sheep that was in fact his own creature, and then ascended into the heights of heaven to offer to the Father and entrust to his care the human race that he had found again. The Lord himself became the firstfruits of the resurrection of mankind, and when its time of punishment for disobedience is over the rest of the body, to which the whole human race belongs, will rise from the grave as the head has done. By God's aid it will grow and be strengthened in all its joints and ligaments, each member having its own proper place in the body. There are many rooms in the Father's house because the body has many members.

God bore with man patiently when he fell because he foresaw the victory that would be his through the Word. Weakness allowed strength its full play, and so revealed God's kindness and great power. ◆

2

Let Us Love One Another

THE NEW COMMANDMENT

Saint Augustine, Bishop

[*From a Treatise on John*]

A new commandment I give you, that you love one another. This commandment that he is giving them is a new one, the Lord Jesus tells his disciples. Yet was it not contained in the Old Law, where it is written: *You shall love your neighbor as yourself?* Why does the Lord call it new when it is clearly so old? Or is the commandment new because it divests us of our former selves and clothes us with the new man? Love does indeed renew the man who hears, or rather obeys its command; but only that love which Jesus distinguished from a natural love by the qualification: *As I have loved you.*

This is the kind of love that renews us. When we love as he loved us we become new men, heirs of the new covenant and singers of the new song. My brothers, this was the love that even in bygone days renewed the holy men, the patriarchs and prophets of old. In later times it renewed the blessed apostles, and now it is the turn of the Gentiles. From the entire human race throughout the world this love gathers together into one body a new people, to be the bride of God's only Son. She is the bride of whom it is asked in the Song of Songs: *Who is this who comes clothed in white?* White indeed are her garments, for she has been made new; and the source of her renewal is none other than this new commandment.

And so all her members make each other's welfare their common care. When one member suffers, all the members suffer with him, and if one member is glorified all the rest rejoice. They hear and obey the Lord's words: *A new commandment I give you, that you love one another*; not as men love one another for their own selfish ends, nor merely on account of their common humanity, but because they are all gods and sons of the Most High. They love one another as God loves them so that they may be brothers of his only Son. He will lead them to the goal that alone will satisfy them, where all their desires will be fulfilled. For when God is all in all, there will be nothing left to desire.

This love is the gift of the Lord who said: *As I have loved you, you also must love one another.* His object in loving us, then, was to enable us to love each other. By loving us himself, our mighty head has linked us all together as members of his own body, bound to one another by the tender bond of love. ❧

CHRIST, THE MODEL
OF BROTHERLY LOVE

Saint Aelred, Abbot

[*From the Mirror of Love*]

The perfection of brotherly love lies in the love of one's enemies. We can find no greater inspiration for this than grateful remembrance of the wonderful patience of Christ. He who is *more fair than all the sons of men* offered his fair face to be spat upon by sinful men; he allowed those eyes that rule the universe to be blindfolded by wicked men; he bared his back to the scourges; he submitted that head which strikes terror in principalities and powers to the sharpness of the thorns; he gave himself up to be mocked and reviled, and at the end endured the cross, the nails, the lance, the gall, the vinegar, remaining always gentle, meek and full of peace.

In short, *he was led like a sheep to the slaughter, and like a lamb before the shearers he kept silent, and did not open his mouth.*

Who could listen to that wonderful prayer, so full of warmth, of love, of unshakable serenity—*Father, forgive them*—and hesitate to embrace his enemies with overflowing love? *Father*, he says, *forgive them*. Is any gentleness, any love, lacking in this prayer?

Yet he put into it something more. It was not enough to pray for them: he wanted also to make excuses for them. *Father, forgive them, for they do not know what they are doing.* They are great sinners, yes, but they have little judgment; therefore, *Father, forgive them*. They are nailing me to the cross, but they do not know who it is that they are nailing to the cross: *if they had known, they would never have crucified the Lord of glory;* therefore, *Father, forgive them*. They think it is a lawbreaker, an impostor claiming to be God, a seducer of the people. I have hidden my face from them, and they do not recognize my glory; therefore, *Father, forgive them, for they do not know what they are doing.*

If someone wishes to love himself he must not allow himself to be corrupted by indulging his sinful nature. If he wishes to resist the promptings of his sinful nature he must enlarge the whole horizon of his love to contemplate the loving gentleness of the humanity of the Lord. Further, if he wishes to savor the joy of brotherly love with greater perfection and delight, he must extend even to his enemies the embrace of true love.

But if he wishes to prevent this fire of divine love from growing cold because of injuries received, let him keep the eyes of his soul always fixed on the serene patience of his beloved Lord and Savior. ∾

DIVINE AND HUMAN MERCY

Saint Caesarius of Arles, Bishop

[*From a Sermon*]

Blessed are the merciful, for they shall receive mercy.
My brothers and sisters, sweet is the thought of mercy,

but even more so is mercy itself. It is what all men hope for, but unfortunately, not what all men deserve. For while all men wish to receive it, only a few are willing to give it.

How can a man ask for himself what he refuses to give to another? If he expects to receive any mercy in heaven, he should give mercy on earth. Do we all desire to receive mercy? Let us make mercy our patroness now, and she will free us in the world to come. Yes, there is mercy in heaven, but the road to it is paved by our merciful acts on earth. As Scripture says: *Lord, your mercy is in heaven.*

There is, therefore, an earthly as well as heavenly mercy, that is to say, a human and a divine mercy. Human mercy has compassion on the miseries of the poor. Divine mercy grants forgiveness of sins. Whatever human mercy bestows here on earth, divine mercy will return to us in our homeland. In this life God feels cold and hunger in all who are stricken with poverty; for, remember, he once said: *What you have done to the least of my brothers you have done to me.* Yes, God who sees fit to give his mercy in heaven wishes it to be a reality here on earth.

What kind of people are we? When God gives, we wish to receive, but when he begs, we refuse to give. Remember, it was Christ who said: *I was hungry and you gave me nothing to eat.* When the poor are starving, Christ too hungers. Do not neglect to improve the unhappy conditions of the poor, if you wish to ensure that your own sins be forgiven you. Christ hungers now, my brethren; it is he who deigns to hunger and thirst in the persons of the poor. And what he will return in heaven tomorrow is what he receives here on earth today.

What do you wish for, what do you pray for, my dear brothers and sisters, when you come to church? Is it mercy? How can it be anything else? Show mercy, then, while you are on earth, and mercy will be shown to you in heaven. A poor person asks you for something; you ask God for something. He begs for a morsel of food; you beg for eternal life. Give to the beggar so that you may merit to receive from Christ. For he it is who says: *Give and it will be given to you.* It baffles me that you have the impudence to ask for what you do not want to give. Give when you come to church. Give to the poor. Give them whatever your resources will allow. ❧

THE DOUBLE COMMANDMENT
OF LOVE

Saint Augustine, Bishop

[*From a Treatise on John*]

The Lord, the teacher of love, full of love, came in person *with summary judgment on the world*, as had been foretold of him, and showed that the law and the prophets are summed up in two commandments of love.

Call to mind, brethren, what these two commandments are. They ought to be very familiar to you; they should not only spring to mind when I mention them, but ought never to be absent from your hearts. Keep always in mind that we must love God and our neighbor: *Love God with your whole heart, your whole soul, and your whole mind, and your neighbor as yourself.*

These two commandments must be always in your thoughts and in your hearts, treasured, acted on, fulfilled. Love of God is the first to be commanded, but love of neighbor is the first to be put into practice. In giving two commandments of love Christ would not commend to you first your neighbor and then God but first God and then your neighbor.

Since you do not yet see God, you merit the vision of God by loving your neighbor. By loving your neighbor you prepare your eye to see God: Saint John says clearly: *If you do not love your brother whom you see, how will you love God whom you do not see!*

Consider what is said to you: Love God. If you say to me: Show me whom I am to love, what shall I say if not what Saint John says: *No one has ever seen God!* But in case you should think that you are completely cut off from the sight of God, he says: *God is love, and he who remains in love remains in God.* Love your neighbor, then, and see within yourself the power by which you love your neighbor; there you will see God, as far as you are able.

Begin, then, to love your neighbor. *Break your bread to feed the hungry, and bring into your home the homeless poor; if you see someone naked, clothe him, and do not look down on your own flesh and blood.*

What will you gain by doing this? *Your light will then burst forth like the dawn.* Your light is your God; he is your *dawn,* for he will come to you when the night of time is over. He does not rise or set but remains for ever.

In loving your neighbor and caring for him you are on a journey. Where are you traveling if not to the Lord

God, to him whom we should love with our whole heart, our whole soul, our whole mind? We have not yet reached his presence, but we have our neighbor at our side. Support, then, this companion of your pilgrimage if you want to come into the presence of the one with whom you desire to remain for ever. ❦

THE ABILITY TO LOVE IS WITHIN EACH OF US

Saint Basil the Great, Bishop

[*From the Detailed Rules for Monks*]

Love of God is not something that can be taught. We did not learn from someone else how to rejoice in light or want to live, or to love our parents or guardians. It is the same—perhaps even more so—with our love for God: it does not come by another's teaching. As soon as the living creature (that is, man) comes to be, a power of reason is implanted in us like a seed, containing within it the ability and the need to love. When the school of God's law admits this power of reason, it cultivates it diligently, skillfully nurtures it, and with God's help brings it to perfection.

For this reason, as by God's gift, I find you with the zeal necessary to attain this end, and you on your part help me with your prayers. I will try to fan into flame the spark of divine love that is hidden within you, as far as I am able through the power of the Holy Spirit.

First, let me say that we have already received from God the ability to fulfill all his commands. We have then no reason to resent them, as if something beyond our capacity were being asked of us. We have no reason either to be angry, as if we had to pay back more than we had received. When we use this ability in a right and fitting way, we lead a life of virtue and holiness. But if we misuse it, we fall into sin.

This is the definition of sin: the misuse of powers given us by God for doing good, a use contrary to God's commandments. On the other hand, the virtue that God asks of us is the use of the same powers based on a good conscience in accordance with God's commands.

Since this is so, we can say the same about love. Since we received a command to love God, we possess from the first moment of our existence an innate power and ability to love. The proof of this is not to be sought outside ourselves, but each one can learn this from himself and in himself. It is natural for us to want things that are good and pleasing to the eye, even though at first different things seem beautiful and good to different people. In the same way, we love what is related to us or near to us, though we have not been taught to do so, and we spontaneously feel well disposed to our benefactors.

What, I ask, is more wonderful than the beauty of God? What thought is more pleasing and satisfying than God's majesty? What desire is as urgent and overpowering as the desire implanted by God in a soul that is completely purified of sin and cries out in its love: *I am wounded by love?* The radiance of the divine beauty is altogether beyond the power of words to describe.

Let Us Sing to the Lord
a Song of Love

Saint Augustine, Bishop

[*From a Sermon*]

S*ing to the Lord a new song; his praise is in the assembly of the saints.* We are urged to sing a new song to the Lord, as new men who have learned a new song. A song is a thing of joy; more profoundly, it is a thing of love. Anyone, therefore, who has learned to love the new life has learned to sing a new song, and the new song reminds us of our new life. The new man, the new song, the new covenant, all belong to the one kingdom of God, and so the new man will sing a new song and will belong to the new covenant.

There is not one who does not love something, but the question is, what to love. The psalms do not tell us not to love, but to choose the object of our love. But how can we choose unless we are first chosen? We cannot love unless someone has loved us first. Listen to the apostle John: *We love him, because he first loved us.* The source of man's love for God can only be found in the fact that God loved him first. He has given us himself as the object of our love, and he has also given us its source. What this source is you may learn more clearly from the apostle Paul who tells us: *The love of God has been poured into our hearts*. This love is not something we generate ourselves; it comes to us *through the Holy Spirit who has been given to us*.

Since we have such an assurance, then, let us love God with the love he has given us. As John tells us more fully: *God is love, and whoever dwells in love dwells in God, and God in him*. It is not enough to say: *Love is from God*. Which of us would dare to pronounce the words of Scripture: *God is love?* He alone could say it who knew what it was to have God dwelling within him. God offers us a short route to the possession of himself. He cries out: Love me and you will have me for you would be unable to love me if you did not possess me already.

My dear brothers and sons, fruit of the true faith and holy seed of heaven, all you who have been born again in Christ and whose life is from above, listen to me; or rather, listen to the Holy Spirit saying through me: *Sing to the Lord a new song*. Look, you tell me, I am singing. Yes indeed, you are singing; you are singing clearly. I can hear you. But make sure that your life does not contradict your words. Sing with your voices, your hearts, your lips and your lives: *Sing to the Lord a new song.*

Now it is your unquestioned desire to sing of him whom you love, but you ask me how to sing his praises. You have heard the words: *Sing to the Lord a new song*, and you wish to know what praises to sing. The answer is: *His praise is in the assembly of the saints;* it is in the singers themselves. If you desire to praise him, then live what you express. Live good lives, and you ourselves will be his praise. ❧

3

Faith in Action

BE SHEPHERDS LIKE THE LORD

Saint Asterius of Amasea, Bishop

[From a Homily]

Y ou were made in the image of God. If then you wish to resemble him, follow his example. Since the very name you bear as Christians is a profession of love for men, imitate the love of Christ.

Reflect for a moment on the wealth of his kindness. Before he came as a man to be among men, he sent John the Baptist to preach repentance and lead men to practice it. John himself was preceded by the prophets, who were to teach the people to repent, to return to God and to amend their lives. Then Christ came himself, and with his own lips cried out: *Come to me, all you who labor and are overburdened, and I will give you rest.* How did he receive those who listened to his call? He readily forgave them their sins; he freed them instantly from all that troubled them. The Word made them holy; the Spirit set his seal on them. The old Adam was buried in the waters of baptism; the new man was reborn to the vigor of grace.

What was the result? Those who had been God's enemies became his friends, those estranged from him became his sons, those who did not know him came to worship and love him.

Let us then be shepherds like the Lord. We must meditate on the Gospel, and as we see in this mirror the example of zeal and loving kindness, we should become thoroughly schooled in these virtues.

For there, obscurely, in the form of a parable, we see a shepherd who had a hundred sheep. When one of them was separated from the flock and lost its way, that shepherd did not remain with the sheep who kept together at pasture. No, he went off to look for the stray. He crossed many valleys and thickets, he climbed great and towering mountains, he spent much time and labor in wandering through solitary places until at last he found his sheep.

When he found it, he did not chastise it; he did not use rough blows to drive it back, but gently placed it on his own shoulders and carried it back to the flock. He took greater joy in this one sheep, lost and found, than in all the others.

Let us look more closely at the hidden meaning of this parable. The sheep is more than a sheep, the shepherd more than a shepherd. They are examples enshrining holy truths. They teach us that we should not look on men as lost or beyond hope; we should not abandon them when they are in danger or be slow to come to their help. When they turn away from the right path and wander, we must lead them back, and rejoice at their return, welcoming them back into the company of those who lead good and holy lives. ∾

SERVE CHRIST IN THE POOR

Saint Gregory of Nazianzen, Bishop

[*From a Sermon*]

B*lessed are the merciful, because they shall obtain mercy*, says the Scripture. Mercy is not the least of the beatitudes. Again: *Blessed is he who is considerate to the needy and the poor*. Once more: *Generous is the man who is merciful and lends*. In another place: *All day the* *just man is merciful and lends.* Let us lay hold of this blessing, let us earn the name of being considerate, let us be generous.

Not even night should interrupt you in your duty of mercy. Do not say: *Come back and I will give you something tomorrow.* There should be no delay between your intention and your good deed. Generosity is the one thing that cannot admit of delay.

Share your bread with the hungry, and bring the needy and the homeless into your house, with a joyful and eager heart. *He who does acts of mercy should do so with cheerfulness.* The grace of a good deed is doubled when it is done with promptness and speed. What is given with a bad grace or against one's will is distasteful and far from praiseworthy.

When we perform an act of kindness we should rejoice and not be sad about it. *If you undo the shackles and the thongs,* says Isaiah, that is, if you do away with miserliness and counting the cost, with hesitation and grumbling, what will be the result? Something great and wonderful! What a marvelous reward there will be: *Your light will break forth like the dawn, and your healing will rise up quickly.* Who would not aspire to light and healing.

If you think that I have something to say, servants of Christ, his brethren and coheirs, let us visit Christ whenever we may; let us care for him, feed him, clothe him, welcome him, honor him, not only at a meal, as some have done, or by anointing him, as Mary did, or only by lending him a tomb, like Joseph of Arimathaea, or by arranging for his burial, like Nicodemus, who loved Christ half-heartedly, or by giving him gold, frankincense and myrrh, like the Magi before all these others. The Lord of all asks for mercy, not sacrifice, and mercy is greater than myriads of fattened lambs. Let us then show him mercy in the persons of the poor and those who today are lying on the ground, so that when we come to leave this world they may receive us into everlasting dwelling places, in Christ our Lord himself, to whom be glory for ever and ever. Amen. ☙

CHRIST SHOULD BE MANIFEST
IN OUR WHOLE LIFE

Saint Gregory of Nyssa, Bishop

[*From a Treatise on Christian Perfection*]

The life of the Christian has three distinguishing aspects: deeds, words and thought. Thought comes first, then words, since our words express openly the interior conclusions of the mind. Finally, after thoughts and words, comes action, for our deeds carry out what the mind has conceived. So when one of these results in our acting or speaking or thinking, we must make sure that all our thoughts, words and deeds are controlled by the divine ideal, the revelation of Christ. For then our thoughts, words and deeds will not fall short of the nobility of their implications.

What then must we do, we who have been found worthy of the name of Christ? Each of us must examine his thoughts, words and deeds, to see whether they are directed toward Christ or are turned away from him. This examination is carried out in various ways. Our deeds or our thoughts or our words are not in harmony with

Christ if they issue from passion. They then bear the mark of the enemy who smears the pearl of the heart with the slime of passion, dimming and even destroying the luster of the precious stone.

On the other hand, if they are free from and untainted by every passionate inclination, they are directed toward Christ, the author and source of peace. He is like a pure, untainted stream. If you draw from him the thoughts in your mind and the inclinations of your heart, you will show a likeness to Christ, your source and origin, as the gleaming water in a jar resembles the flowing water from which it was obtained.

For the purity of Christ and the purity that is manifest in our hearts are identical. Christ's purity, however, is the fountainhead; ours has its source in him and flows out of him. Our life is stamped with the beauty of his thought. The inner and the outer man are harmonized in a kind of music. The mind of Christ is the controlling influence that inspires us to moderation and goodness in our behavior. As I see it, Christian perfection consists in this: sharing the titles which express the meaning of Christ's name, we bring out this meaning in our minds, our prayers and our way of life. ◠

THE CHRISTIAN IN THE WORLD

[*From a Letter to Diognetus*]

Christians are indistinguishable from other men either by nationality, language or customs. They do not inhabit separate cities of their own, or speak a strange dialect, or follow some outlandish way of life. Their teaching is not based upon reveries inspired by the curiosity of men. Unlike some other people, they champion no purely human doctrine. With regard to dress, food and manner of life in general, they follow the customs of whatever city they happen to be living in, whether it is Greek or foreign.

And yet there is something extraordinary about their lives. They live in their own countries as though they were only passing through. They play their full role as citizens, but labor under all the disabilities of aliens. Any country can be their homeland, but for them their homeland, wherever it may be, is a foreign country. Like others, they marry and have children, but they do not expose them. They share their meals, but not their wives. They live in the flesh, but they are not governed by the desires of the flesh. They pass their days upon earth, but they are citizens of heaven. Obedient to the laws, they yet live on a level that transcends the law.

Christians love all men, but all men persecute them. Condemned because they are not understood, they are put to death, but raised to life again. They live in poverty, but enrich many; they are totally destitute, but possess an abundance of everything. They suffer dishonor, but that is their glory. They are defamed, but vindicated. A blessing is their answer to abuse, deference their response to insult. For the good they do they receive the punishment of malefactors, but even then they rejoice, as though receiving the gift of life. They are attacked by the Jews as aliens, they are persecuted by the Greeks, yet no one can explain the reason for this hatred.

To speak in general terms, we may say that the Christian is to the world what the soul is to the body. As the soul is present in every part of the body, while remaining distinct from it, so Christians are found in all the cities of the world, but cannot be identified with the world. As the visible body contains the invisible soul, so Christians are seen living in the world, but their religious life remains unseen. The body hates the soul and wars against it, not because of any injury the soul has done it, but because of the restriction the soul places on its pleasures. Similarly, the world hates the Christians, not because they have done it any wrong, but because they are opposed to its enjoyments.

Christians love those who hate them just as the soul loves the body and all its members despite the body's hatred. It is by the soul, enclosed within the body, that the body is held together, and similarly, it is by the Christians, detained in the world as in a prison, that the world is held together. The soul, though immortal, has a mortal dwelling place; and Christians also live for a time amidst perishable things, while awaiting the freedom from change and decay that will be theirs in heaven. As the soul benefits from the deprivation of food and drink, so Christians flourish under persecution. Such is the Christian's lofty and divinely appointed function, from which he is not permitted to excuse himself. ❧

THE LIGHT OF A CHRISTIAN CANNOT ESCAPE NOTICE

Saint John Chrysostom, Bishop

[*From a Homily on the Acts of the Apostles*]

There is nothing colder than a Christian who does not seek to save others.

You cannot plead poverty here; the widow putting in her two small coins will be your accuser. Peter said: *Silver and gold I have not.* Paul was so poor that he was often hungry and went without necessary food.

You cannot plead humble birth, for they were humbly born, of humble stock. You cannot offer the excuse of lack of education, for they were uneducated. You cannot plead ill-health, for Timothy also had poor health, with frequent illnesses.

Each one can help his neighbor if only he is willing to do what is in his power. Look at the trees that do not bear fruit: have you not noticed how strong and fine they are, upstanding, smooth and tall? If we had a garden, we would much prefer trees with fruit—pomegranates and olives—to trees that are for pleasure, not for utility, and any utility these have is small.

Such are those men who think only of their own concerns. In fact, they are even worse: the trees are at least useful for building or for protection, whereas the selfish are fit only for punishment. Such were those foolish virgins who were chaste, comely and self-controlled, but did nothing for anyone. So they are consumed in the fire. Such are those men who refuse to give Christ food.

Notice that none of them is accused of personal sins. They are not accused of committing fornication or perjury or any such sin at all: only of not helping anybody else. The man who buried the talent was like this. His life was blameless, but he was of no service to others.

How can such a person be a Christian? Tell me, if yeast did not make the whole mass like itself, is it really yeast? Again, if perfume failed to pervade all around it with its fragrance, would we call it perfume?

Do not say: it is impossible for me to influence others. If you are a Christian, it is impossible for this not to happen. Things found in nature cannot be denied; so here, for it is a question of the nature of the Christian.

Do not insult God. If you say that the sun cannot shine, you have insulted him. If you say that a Christian cannot help others, you have insulted God and called him a liar. It is easier for the sun not to give warmth or shine than for the Christian not to shed his light. It is easier for light to be darkness than for this to happen.

Do not say then that it is impossible. The opposite is impossible. Do not insult God. If we have put our affairs in order, these things will certainly come to be, and will follow as a natural consequence. The light of a Christian cannot escape notice. So bright a lamp cannot be hidden. ∾

4

Walking in the Light

WE POSSESS CHRIST,
OUR PEACE, OUR LIGHT

Saint Gregory of Nyssa, Bishop

[*From a Treatise on Christian Perfection*]

*H*e is our peace, for he has made both one. Since we think of Christ as our peace, we may call ourselves true Christians only if our lives express Christ by our own peace. As the Apostle says: *He has put enmity to death.* We must never allow it to be rekindled in us in any way but must declare that it is absolutely dead. Gloriously has God slain enmity, in order to save us; may we never risk the life of our souls by being resentful or by bearing grudges. We must not awaken that enmity or call it back to life by our wickedness, for it is better left dead.

No, since we possess Christ who is peace, we must put an end to this enmity and live as we believe he lived. He broke down the separating wall, uniting what was divided, bringing about peace by reconciling in his single person those who disagreed. In the same way, we must be reconciled not only with those who attack us from outside, but also with those who stir up dissension within; flesh then will no longer be opposed to the spirit, nor the spirit to the flesh. Once we subject the wisdom of the flesh to God's law, we shall be re-created as one single man at peace. Then, having become one instead of two, we shall have peace within ourselves.

Now peace is defined as harmony among those who are divided. When, therefore, we end that civil war within our nature and cultivate peace within ourselves, we become peace. By this peace we demonstrate that the name of Christ, which we bear, is authentic and appropriate.

When we consider that Christ is the true light, having nothing in common with deceit, we learn that our own life also must shine with the rays of that true light. Now these rays of the Sun of Justice are the virtues which pour out to enlighten us so that *we may put away the works of darkness and walk honorably as in broad daylight.* When we reject the deeds of darkness and do everything in the light of day, we become light and, as light should, we give light to others by our actions.

If we truly think of Christ as our source of holiness, we shall refrain from anything wicked or impure in thought or act and thus show ourselves to be worthy bearers of his name. For the quality of holiness is shown not by what we say but by what we do in life. ⬳

THE MEANING OF "THE FEAR OF THE LORD"

Saint Hilary, Bishop

[*From a Treatise on the Psalms*]

*B*lessed are those who fear the Lord, who walk in his *ways*. Notice that when Scripture speaks of the fear of the Lord it does not leave the phrase in isolation, as if it were a complete summary of faith. No, many things are added to it, or are presupposed by it. From these we may learn its meaning and excellence. In the book of Proverbs Solomon tells us: *If you cry out for wisdom and raise your voice for understanding, if you look for it as for silver and search for it as for treasure,* *then you will understand the fear of the Lord.* We see here the difficult journey we must undertake before we can arrive at the fear of the Lord.

We must begin by crying out for wisdom. We must hand over to our intellect the duty of making every decision. We must look for wisdom and search for it. Then we must understand the fear of the Lord.

"Fear" is not to be taken in the sense that common usage gives it. Fear in this ordinary sense is the trepidation our weak humanity feels when it is afraid of suffering something it does not want to happen. We are afraid, or are made afraid, because of a guilty conscience, the rights of someone more powerful, an attack from one who is stronger, sickness, encountering a wild beast, suffering evil in any form. This kind of fear is not taught: it happens because we are weak. We do not have to learn what we should fear: objects of fear bring their own terror with them.

But of the fear of the Lord this is what is written: *Come, my children, listen to me, I shall teach you the fear of the Lord.* The fear of the Lord has then to be learned because it can be taught. It does not lie in terror, but in something that can be taught. It does not arise from the fearfulness of our nature; it has to be acquired by obedience to the commandments, by holiness of life and by knowledge of the truth.

For us the fear of God consists wholly in love, and perfect love of God brings our fear of him to its perfection. Our love for God is entrusted with its own responsibility: to observe his counsels, to obey his laws, to trust his promises. Let us hear what Scripture says: *And now, Israel, what does the Lord your God ask of you except to fear the Lord your God and walk in all his ways and love him and keep his commandments with your whole heart and your whole soul, so that it may be well for you?*

The ways of the Lord are many, though he is himself the way. When he speaks of himself he calls himself the way and shows us the reason why he called himself the way: *No one can come to the Father except through me.*

We must ask for these many ways, we must travel along these many ways, to find the one that is good. That is, we shall find the one way of eternal life through the guidance of many teachers. These ways are found in the law, in the prophets, in the gospels, in the writings of the apostles, in the different good works by which we fulfill the commandments. Blessed are those who walk these ways in the fear of the Lord. ❧

SINCERE REPENTANCE

[*From a Homily Written in the Second Century*]

We should repent of our sins while we are still on earth. When a potter is making a vessel and it becomes misshapen or breaks in his hands, he shapes it again; but once placed in the oven, it is beyond repair. Now the clay in the craftsman's hands is an image of ourselves, and it teaches us that, while still in this world, we must wholeheartedly repent of sins committed in the body and make it possible for the Lord to save us while there is time. When we have left this world, we shall no longer be able to repent and confess our sins. We must do the will of the Father, keep our bodies pure, and observe the commandments of the Lord, for this is the way to obtain eternal life. The Lord says in the gospel: *If you have not been observant in small matters, who will entrust you with anything important? For I tell you that the man who is faithful in the smallest things is faithful in the greatest things as well.* In other words, in order to obtain eternal life, we must remain pure and keep the seal of our baptism undefiled.

Nor must any of you say that our bodies will not share in the judgment, nor rise again. In what were you saved? In what did you receive your sight? Think for a moment. Was it not in this very body? Our bodies are the temple of God, and as such we must guard them, for even as we were called in the body, so shall we also be judged in the body. Since Christ, our Lord and Savior, who in the beginning was spirit, became flesh and in this way called us, it is in this flesh of ours that we shall also receive our reward.

Therefore, let us love one another, so that we may all attain to the kingdom of God. While we can still be healed, let us surrender ourselves into the hands of our divine physician and give him his recompense—the recompense of true sorrow for our sins. Since he who knows all things sees what is in our hearts, let us praise him with our hearts as well as our lips. He will then receive us as his sons. The Lord himself has said: *Those who do my Father's will are my brothers.*

LET US SHOW EACH OTHER GOD'S GENEROSITY

Saint Gregory of Nazianzen, Bishop

[*From a Sermon*]

Recognize to whom you owe the fact that you exist, that you breathe, that you understand, that you are wise, and, above all, that you know God and hope for the kingdom of heaven and vision of glory, now darkly and as in a mirror but then with greater fullness and purity. You have been made a son of God, coheir with Christ. Where did you get all this, and from whom?

Let me turn to what is of less importance: the visible world around us. What benefactor has enabled you to look out upon the beauty of the sky, the sun in its course, the circle of the moon, the countless number of stars, with the harmony and order that are theirs, like the music of a harp? Who has blessed you with rain, with the art of husbandry, with different kinds of food, with the arts, with houses, with laws, with states, with a life of humanity and culture, with friendship and the easy familiarity of kinship?

Who has given you dominion over animals, those that are tame and those that provide you with food? Who has made you lord and master of everything on earth? In short, who has endowed you with all that makes man superior to all other living creatures?

Is it not God who asks you now in your turn to show yourself generous above all other creatures and for the sake of all other creatures? Because we have received from him so many wonderful gifts, will we not be ashamed to refuse him this one thing only, our generosity? Though he is God and Lord he is not afraid to be known as our Father. Shall we for our part repudiate those who are our kith and kin?

Brethren and friends, let us never allow ourselves to misuse what has been given us by God's gift. If we do, we shall hear Saint Peter say: *Be ashamed of yourselves for holding on to what belongs to someone else. Resolve to imitate God's justice, and no one will be poor.* Let us not labor to heap up and hoard riches while others remain in need. If we do, the prophet Amos will speak out against us with sharp and threatening words: *Come now, you that say: When will the new moon be over, so that we may start selling? When will sabbath be over, so that we may start opening our treasures?*

Let us put into practice the supreme and primary law of God. He sends down rain on just and sinful alike, and causes the sun to rise on all without distinction. To all earth's creatures he has given the broad earth, the springs, the rivers and the forests. He has given the air to the birds, and the waters to those who live in water. He has given abundantly to all the basic needs of life, not as a private possession, not restricted by law, not divided by boundaries, but as common to all, amply and in rich measure. His gifts are not deficient in any way, because he wanted to give equality of blessing to equality of worth, and to show the abundance of his generosity. ✑

FIVE PATHS OF REPENTANCE

Saint John Chrysostom, Bishop

[*From a Homily*]

W ould you like me to list also the paths of repentance? They are numerous and quite varied, and all lead to heaven.

A first path of repentance is the condemnation of your own sins: *Be the first to admit your sins and you will be justified*. For this reason, too, the prophet wrote: *I said: I will accuse myself of my sins to the Lord, and you forgave the wickedness of my heart*. Therefore, you too should condemn your own sins; that will be enough reason for the Lord to forgive you, for a man who condemns his own sins is slower to commit them again. Rouse your conscience to accuse you within your own house, lest it become your accuser before the judgment seat of the Lord.

That, then, is one very good path of repentance. Another and no less valuable one is to put out of our minds the harm done us by our enemies, in order to master our anger, and to forgive our fellow servants' sins against us. Then our own sins against the Lord will be forgiven us. Thus you have another way to atone for sin: *For if you forgive your debtors, your heavenly Father will forgive you*.

Do you want to know of a third path? It consists of prayer that is fervent, careful and comes from the heart.

If you want to hear of a fourth, I will mention almsgiving, whose power is great and far-reaching.

If, moreover, a man lives a modest, humble life, that, no less than the other things I have mentioned, takes sin away. Proof of this is the tax-collector who had no good deeds to mention, but offered his humility instead and was relieved of a heavy burden of sin.

Thus I have shown you five paths of repentance: condemnation of your own sins, forgiveness of our neighbor's sins against us, prayer, almsgiving and humility.

Do not be idle, then, but walk daily in all these paths; they are easy, and you cannot plead your poverty. For, though you live out your life amid great need, you can always set aside your wrath, be humble, pray diligently and condemn your own sins; poverty is no hindrance. Poverty is not an obstacle to our carrying out the Lord's bidding, even when it comes to that path of repentance which involves giving money (almsgiving, I mean). The widow proved that when she put her two mites into the box!

Now that we have learned how to heal these wounds of ours, let us apply the cures. Then, when we have regained genuine health, we can approach the holy table with confidence, go gloriously to meet Christ, the king of glory, and attain the eternal blessings through the grace, mercy and kindness of Jesus Christ, our Lord. ❧

5

Sing a New Song

LET US SING ALLELUIA
TO THE GOOD GOD
WHO DELIVERS US FROM EVI

Saint Augustine, Bishop

[*From a Sermon*]

Let us sing alleluia here on earth, while we still live in anxiety, so that we may sing it one day in heaven in full security. Why do we now live in anxiety? Can you expect me not to feel anxious when I read: *Is not man's life on earth a time of trial?* Can you expect me not to feel anxious when the words still ring in my ears: *Watch and pray that you will not be put to the test?* Can you expect me not to feel anxious when there are so many temptations here below that prayer itself reminds us of them, when we say: *Forgive us our trespasses, as we forgive those who trespass against us?* Every day we make our petitions, every day we sin. Do you want me to feel secure when I am daily asking pardon for my sins, and requesting help in time of trial? Because of my past sins I pray: *Forgive us our trespasses, as we forgive those who trespass against us*, and then, because of the perils still before me, I immediately go on to add: *Lead us not into temptation*. How can all be well with people who are crying out with me: *Deliver us from evil?* And yet, brothers, while we are still in the midst of this evil, let us sing alleluia to the good God who delivers us from evil.

Even here amidst trials and temptations let us, let all men, sing alleluia. *God is faithful*, says holy Scripture, *and he will not allow you to be tried beyond your strength*. So let us sing alleluia, even here on earth. Man is still a debtor, but God is faithful. Scripture does not say that he will not allow you to be tried, but that *he will not allow you to be tried beyond your strength. Whatever the trial, he will see you through it safely, and so enable you to endure.* You have entered upon a time of trial but you will come to no harm—God's help will bring you through it safely. You are like a piece of pottery, shaped by instruction, fired by tribulation. When you are put into the oven therefore, keep your thoughts on the time when you will be taken out again; for God is faithful, and *he will guard both your going in and your coming out.*

But in the next life, when this body of ours has

become immortal and incorruptible, then all trials will be over. *Your body is indeed dead, and why? Because of sin.* Nevertheless, *your spirit lives, because you have been justified.* Are we to leave our dead bodies behind then? By no means. Listen to the words of holy Scripture: *If the Spirit of him who raised Christ from the dead dwells within you, then he who raised Christ from the dead will also give life to your own mortal bodies.* At present your body receives its life from the soul, but then it will receive it from the Spirit.

O the happiness of the heavenly alleluia, sung in security, in fear of no adversity! We shall have no enemies in heaven, we shall never lose a friend. God's praises are sung both there and here, but here they are sung in anxiety, there, in security; here they are sung by those destined to die, there, by those destined to live for ever; here they are sung in hope, there, in hope's fulfillment; here they are sung by wayfarers, there, by those living in their own country.

So, then, my brothers, let us sing now, not in order to enjoy a life of leisure, but in order to lighten our labors. You should sing as wayfarers do—sing, but continue your journey. Do not be lazy, but sing to make your journey more enjoyable. Sing, but keep going. What do I mean by keep going? Keep on making progress. This progress, however, must be in virtue; for there are some, the Apostle warns, whose only progress is in vice. If you make progress, you will be continuing your journey, but be sure that your progress is in virtue, true faith and right living. Sing then, but keep going. ∾

I SHALL SING IN SPIRIT, AND WITH UNDERSTANDING

Saint Ambrose, Bishop

[*From the Explanations of the Psalms*]

What is more pleasing than a psalm? David expresses it well: *Praise the Lord, for a song of praise is good: let there be praise of our God with gladness and grace.* Yes, a psalm is a blessing on the lips of the people, a hymn in praise of God, the assembly's homage, a general acclamation, a word that speaks for all, the voice of the Church, a confession of faith in song. It is the voice of complete assent, the joy of freedom, a cry of happiness, the echo of gladness. It soothes the temper, distracts from care, lightens the burden of sorrow. It is a source of security at night, a lesson in wisdom by day. It is a shield when we are afraid, a celebration of holiness, a vision of serenity, a promise of peace and harmony. It is like a lyre, evoking harmony from a blend of notes. Day begins to the music of a psalm. Day closes to the echo of a psalm.

In a psalm instruction vies with beauty. We sing for pleasure. We learn for our profit. What experience is not covered by a reading of the psalms? I come across the words: *A song for the beloved*, and I am aflame with desire for God's love. I go through God's revelation in all its beauty, the intimations of resurrection, the gifts of his promise. I learn to avoid sin. I see my mistake in feeling ashamed of repentance for my sins.

What is a psalm but a musical instrument to give expression to all the virtues? The psalmist of old used it, with the aid of the Holy Spirit, to make earth reecho the music of heaven. He used the dead gut of strings to create harmony from a variety of notes, in order to send up to heaven the song of God's praise. In doing so he taught us that we must first die to sin, and then create in our lives on earth a harmony through virtuous deeds, if the grace of our devotion is to reach up to the Lord.

David thus taught us that we must sing an interior song of praise, like St. Paul, who tells us: *I shall pray in spirit, and also with understanding; I shall sing in spirit, and also with understanding.* We must fashion our lives and shape our actions in the light of the things that are above. We must not allow pleasure to awaken bodily passions, which weigh our soul down instead of freeing it. The holy prophet told us that his songs of praise were to celebrate the freeing of his soul, when he said: *I shall sing to you, God, on the lyre, holy one of Israel; my lips will rejoice when I have sung to you, and my soul also, which you have set free.* ∾

THE APPEAL OF THE BOOK OF PSALMS

Saint Ambrose, Bishop

[*From the Explanations of the Psalms*]

Though all Scripture is fragrant with God's grace, the Book of Psalms has a special attractiveness.

Moses wrote the history of Israel's forefathers in prose, but after leading the people through the Red Sea—a wonder that remained in their memory—he broke into a song of triumph in praise of God when he saw King Pharaoh drowned along with his forces. His genius soared to a higher level, to match an accomplishment beyond his own powers.

Miriam too raised her timbrel and sang encouragement for the rest of the women, saying: *Let us sing to the Lord, for he has triumphed gloriously; he has cast horse and rider into the sea.*

In the Book of Psalms there is profit for all, with healing power for our salvation. There is instruction from history, teaching from the law, prediction from prophecy, chastisement from denunciation, persuasion from moral preaching. All who read it may find the cure for their own individual failings. All with eyes to see can discover in it a complete gymnasium for the soul, a stadium for all the virtues, equipped for every kind of exercise; it is for each to choose the kind he judges best to help him gain the prize.

If you wish to read and imitate the deeds of the past, you will find the whole history of the Israelites in a single psalm: in one short reading you can amass a treasure for the memory. If you want to study the power of the law, which is summed up in the bond of charity (*Whoever loves his neighbor has fulfilled the law*), you may read in the

psalms of the great love with which one man faced seri-
ous dangers singlehandedly in order to remove the
shame of the whole people. You will find the glory of
charity more than a match for the parade of power.

What am I to say of the grace of prophecy? We
see that what others hinted at in riddles was promised
openly and clearly to the psalmist alone: the Lord
Jesus was to be born of his seed, according to the
word of the Lord, *I will place upon your throne one who
is the fruit of your flesh.*

In the psalms, then, not only is Jesus born for us,
he also undergoes his saving passion in his body, he
lies in death, he rises again, he ascends into heaven,
he sits at the right hand of the Father. What no man
would have dared to say was foretold by the psalmist
alone, and afterward proclaimed by the Lord himself
in the Gospel. ❧

Our Prayer Is Communal

Saint Cyprian, Bishop and Martyr
[*From a Treatise on the Lord's Prayer*]

Above all, he who preaches peace and unity did not want us to pray by ourselves in private or for ourselves alone. We do not say "My Father, who art in heaven," nor "Give me this day my daily bread." It is not for himself alone that each person asks to be forgiven, not to be led into temptation or to be delivered from evil. Rather, we pray in public as a community, and not for one individual but for all. For the people of God are all one.

God is then the teacher of harmony, peace and unity, and desires each of us to pray for all men, even as he bore all men in himself alone. The three young men shut up in the furnace of fire observed this rule of prayer. United in the bond of the Spirit they uttered together the same prayer. The witness of holy Scripture describes this incident for us, so that we might imitate them in our prayer. *Then all three began to sing in unison, blessing God.* Even though Christ had not yet taught them to pray, nevertheless, they spoke as with one voice.

It is for this reason that their prayer was persuasive and efficacious. For their simple and spiritual prayer of peace merited the presence of the Lord. So too, after the ascension we find the apostles and the disciples praying together in this way. Scripture relates: *They all joined together in continuous prayer, with the women including Mary, the mother of Jesus, and his brothers.* They all joined together in continuous prayer. The urgency and the unity of their prayer declares that God, *who fashions a bond of unity among those who live in his home,* will admit into his divine home for all eternity only those who pray in unity.

My dear friends, the Lord's Prayer contains many great mysteries of our faith. In these few words there is great spiritual strength, for this summary of divine teaching contains all of our prayers and petitions. And so, the Lord commands us: *Pray then like this: Our Father, who art in heaven.*

We are new men; we have been reborn and restored to God by his grace. We have already begun to be his sons and we can say "Father." John reminds us of this: *He came to his own home, and his own people did not receive him. But to all who received him, who believe in his name, he gave the power to become children* of God. Profess your belief that you are sons of God by giving thanks. Call upon God who is your Father in heaven. ❧

PRAY ESPECIALLY FOR THE WHOLE BODY OF THE CHURCH

Saint Ambrose, Bishop
[*From a Treatise on Cain and Abel*]

*O*ffer God a sacrifice of praise and fulfill your vows *to the Most High.* If you praise God you offer your vow and fulfill the promise you have made. So the Samaritan leper, healed by the Lord's word of command, gained a greater credit than the other nine; he alone returned to Christ, praising God and giving thanks. Jesus said of him: *There was no one to come back and thank God except this foreigner. He tells him: Stand up and go on your way, for your faith has made you whole.*

The Lord Jesus, in his divine wisdom, taught you about the goodness of the Father, who knows how to give good things, so that you might ask for the things that are good from Goodness itself. He urges you to pray earnestly and frequently, not offering long and wearisome prayers, but praying often, and with perseverance. Lengthy prayers are usually filled with empty words, while neglect of prayer results in indifference to prayer.

Again, Christ urges you, when you ask forgiveness for yourself, to be especially generous to others, so that your actions may commend your prayer. The Apostle, too, teaches you how to pray: you must avoid anger and contentiousness, so that your prayer may be serene and wholesome. He tells you also that every place is a place of prayer, though our Savior says: *Go into your room.*

But by "room" you must understand, not a room enclosed by walls that imprison your body, but the room that is within you, the room where you hide your thoughts, where you keep your affections. This room of prayer is always with you, wherever you are, and it is always a secret room, where only God can see you.

You are told to pray especially for the people, that is, for the whole body, for all its members, the family of your mother the Church; the badge of membership in this body is love for each other. If you pray for yourself, you pray for yourself alone. If each one prays for himself, he receives less from God's goodness than the one who prays on behalf of others. But as it is, because each prays for all, all are in fact praying for each one.

To conclude, if you pray only for yourself, you will be praying, as we said, for yourself alone. But if you pray for all, all will pray for you, for you are included in all. In this way there is a great recompense; through the prayers of each individual, the intercession of the whole people is gained for each individual. There is here no pride, but an increase of humility and a richer harvest from prayer. ◈

LET US EXERCISE OUR DESIRE IN PRAYER

Saint Augustine, Bishop

[*From a Letter to Proba*]

Why in our fear of not praying as we should, do we turn to so many things, to find what we should pray for? Why do we not say instead, in the words of the psalm:

I have asked one thing from the Lord, this is what I will seek: to dwell in the Lord's house all the days of my life, to see the graciousness of the Lord, and to visit his temple. There, the days do not come and go in succession, and the beginning of one day does not mean the end of another; all days are one, simultaneously and without end, and the life lived out in these days has itself no end.

So that we might obtain this life of happiness, he who is true life itself taught us to pray, not in many words as though speaking longer could gain us a hearing. After all, we pray to one who, as the Lord himself tells us, knows what we need before we ask for it.

Why he should ask us to pray, when he knows what we need before we ask him, may perplex us if we do not realize that our Lord and God does not want to know what we want (for he cannot fail to know it) but wants us rather to exercise our desire through our prayers, so that we may be able to receive what he is preparing to give us. His gift is very great indeed, but our capacity is too small and limited to receive it. That is why we are told: *Enlarge your desires, do not bear the yoke with unbelievers.*

The deeper our faith, the stronger our hope, the greater our desire, the larger will be our capacity to receive that gift, which is very great indeed. *No eye has seen it;* it has no color. *No ear has heard it;* it has no sound. *It has not entered man's heart;* man's heart must enter into it.

In this faith, hope and love we pray always with unwearied desire. However, at set times and seasons we also pray to God in words, so that by these signs we may instruct ourselves and mark the progress we have made in our desire, and spur ourselves on to deepen it. The more fervent the desire, the more worthy will be its fruit. When the Apostle tells us: *Pray without ceasing,* he means this: Desire unceasingly that life of happiness which is nothing if not eternal, and ask it of him who alone is able to give it. ❧

On the Lord's Prayer

Saint Augustine, Bishop

[*From a Letter to Proba*]

We need to use words so that we may remind ourselves to consider carefully what we are asking, not so that we may think we can instruct the Lord or prevail on him.

Thus, when we say: *Hallowed be your name*, we are reminding ourselves to desire that his name, which in fact is always holy, should also be considered holy among men. I mean that it should not be held in contempt. But this is a help for men, not for God.

And as for our saying: *Your kingdom come*, it will surely come whether we will it or not. But we are stirring up our desires for the kingdom so that it can come to us and we can deserve to reign there.

When we say: *Your will be done on earth as it is in heaven*, we are asking him to make us obedient so that his will may be done in us as it is done in heaven by his angels.

When we say: *Give us this day our daily bread*, in saying *this day* we mean "in this world." Here we ask for a sufficiency by specifying the most important part of it; that is, we use the word "bread" to stand for everything. Or else we are asking for the sacrament of the faithful, which is necessary in this world, not to gain temporal happiness but to gain the happiness that is everlasting.

When we say: *Forgive us our trespasses as we forgive those who trespass against us*, we are reminding ourselves of what we must ask and what we must do in order to be worthy in turn to receive.

When we say: *Lead us not into temptation*, we are reminding ourselves to ask that his help may not depart from us; otherwise we could be seduced and consent to some temptation, or despair and yield to it.

When we say: *Deliver us from evil*, we are reminding ourselves to reflect on the fact that we do not yet enjoy the state of blessedness in which we shall suffer no evil. This is the final petition contained in the Lord's Prayer, and it has a wide application. In this petition the Christian can utter his cries of sorrow, in it he can shed his tears, and through it he can begin, continue and conclude his prayer, whatever the distress in which he finds himself. Yes, it was very appropriate that all these truths should be entrusted to us to remember in these very words.

Whatever be the other words we may prefer to say (words which the one praying chooses so that his disposition may become clearer to himself or which he simply adopts so that his disposition may be intensified), we say nothing that is not contained in the Lord's Prayer, provided of course we are praying in a correct and proper way. But if anyone says something which is incompatible with this prayer of the Gospel, he is praying in the flesh, even if he is not praying sinfully. And yet I do not know how this could be termed anything but sinful, since those who are born again through the Spirit ought to pray only in the Spirit. ❧

6

The Bond of Unity

THE PRESERVATION OF UNITY

Saint Clement I, Pope

[*From a Letter to the Corinthians*]

Beloved, Jesus Christ is our salvation, he is the high priest through whom we present our offerings and the helper who supports us in our weakness. Through him our gaze penetrates the heights of heaven and we see, as in a mirror, the most holy face of God. Through Christ the eyes of our hearts are opened, and our weak and clouded understanding reaches up toward the light. Through him the Lord God willed that we should taste eternal knowledge, for Christ *is the radiance of God's glory, and as much greater than the angels as the name God has given him is superior to theirs.*

So then, my brothers, let us do battle with all our might under his unerring command. Think of the men serving under our military commanders. How well disciplined they are! How readily and submissively they carry out orders! Not everyone can be a prefect, a tribune, a centurion, or a captain of fifty, but each man in his own rank executes the orders of the emperor and the officers in command. The great cannot exist without those of humble condition, nor can those of humble condition exist without the great. Always it is the harmonious working together of its various parts that insures the well-being of the whole. Take our own body as an example: the head is helpless without the feet; and the feet can do nothing without the head. Even our least important members are useful and necessary to the whole body, and all work together for its well-being in harmonious subordination.

Let us, then, preserve the unity of the body that we form in Christ Jesus, and let everyone give his neighbor the deference to which his particular gifts entitle him. Let the strong care for the weak and the weak respect the strong. Let the wealthy assist the poor and the poor man thank God for giving him someone to supply his needs. The wise man should show his wisdom not by his eloquence but by good works; the humble man should not proclaim his own humility, but leave others to do so; nor must the man who preserves his chastity ever boast of it, but recognize that the ability to control his desires has been given him by another.

Think, my brothers, of how we first came into being, of what we were at the first moment of our existence. Think of the dark tomb out of which our Creator brought us into his world where he had his gifts prepared for us even before we were born. All this we owe to him and for everything we must give him thanks. To him be glory for ever and ever. Amen. ⟨⟩

THE WORD CREATES A DIVINE HARMONY IN CREATION

Saint Athanasius, Bishop

[*From a Discourse "Against the Pagans"*]

I*n the beginning was the Word, and the Word was with God, and the Word was God. All things were made through him, and without him nothing was made.* In these words John the theologian teaches that nothing exists or remains in being except in and through the Word.

Think of a musician tuning his lyre. By his skill he adjusts high notes to low and intermediate notes to the rest, and produces a series of harmonies. So too the wisdom of God holds the world like a lyre and joins things in the air to those on earth, and things in heaven to those in the air, and brings each part into harmony with the whole. By his decree and will he regulates them all to produce the beauty and harmony of a single, well-ordered universe. While remaining unchanged with his Father, he moves all creation by his unchanging nature, according to the Father's will. To everything he gives existence and life in accordance with its nature, and so creates a wonderful and truly divine harmony.

To illustrate this profound mystery, let us take the example of a choir of many singers. A choir is composed of a variety of men, women and children, of both old and young. Under the direction of one conductor, each sings in the way that is natural for him: men with men's voices, boys with boys' voices, old people with old voices, young people with young voices. Yet all of them produce a single harmony. Or consider the example of our soul. It moves our senses according to their several functions so that in the presence of a single object they all act simultaneously: the eye sees, the ear hears, the hand touches, the nose smells, the tongue tastes, and often the other parts of the body act as well as, for example, the feet may walk.

Although this is only a poor comparison, it gives some idea of how the whole universe is governed. The Word of God has but to give a gesture of command and everything falls into place; each creature performs its own proper function, and all together constitute one single harmonious order. ❧

I Am the Vine, You Are the Branches

Saint Cyril of Alexandria, Bishop

[*From a Commentary on the Gospel of John*]

The Lord calls himself the vine and those united to him branches in order to teach us how much we shall benefit from our union with him, and how important it is for us to remain in his love. By receiving the Holy Spirit, who is the bond of union between us and Christ our Savior, those who are joined to him, as branches are to a vine, share in his own nature.

On the part of those who come to the vine, their union with him depends upon a deliberate act of the will; on his part, the union is effected by grace. Because we had good will, we made the act of faith that brought us to Christ, and received from him the dignity of adoptive sonship that made us his own kinsmen, according to the words of Saint Paul: *He who is joined to the Lord is one spirit with him.*

The prophet Isaiah calls Christ the foundation, because it is upon him that we as living and spiritual stones are built into a holy priesthood to be a dwelling place for God in the Spirit. Upon no other foundation than Christ can this temple be built. Here Christ is teaching the same truth by calling himself the vine, since the vine is the parent of its branches, and provides their nourishment.

From Christ and in Christ, we have been reborn through the Spirit in order to bear the fruit of life; not the fruit of our old, sinful life but the fruit of a new life founded upon our faith in him and our love for him. Like branches growing from a vine, we now draw our life from Christ, and we cling to his holy commandment in order to preserve this life. Eager to safeguard the blessing of our noble birth, we are careful not to grieve the Holy Spirit who dwells in us, and who makes us aware of God's presence in us.

Let the wisdom of John teach us how we live in Christ and Christ lives in us: *The proof that we are living in him and he is living in us is that he has given us a share in his Spirit.* Just as the trunk of the vine gives its own natural properties to each of its branches, so, by bestowing on them the Holy Spirit, the Word of God, the only-begotten Son of the Father, gives Christians a certain kinship with himself and with God the Father because they have been united to him by faith and determination to do his will in all things. He helps them to grow in love and reverence for God, and teaches them to discern right from wrong and to act with integrity. ༄

THE SACRAMENT OF UNITY AND LOVE

Saint Fulgentius of Ruspe, Bishop

[*From a Book Addressed to Monimus*]

The spiritual building up of the body of Christ is achieved through love. As Saint Peter says: *Like living stones you are built into a spiritual house, to be a holy priesthood, offering spiritual sacrifices acceptable to God through Jesus Christ.* And there can be no more effective way to pray for this spiritual growth than for the Church, itself Christ's body, to make the offering of his body and blood in the sacramental form of bread and wine. *For the cup we drink is a participation in the blood of Christ, and the bread we break is a participation in the body of Christ. Because there is one loaf, we who are many are one body, since we all share the same bread.* And so we pray that, by the same grace which made the Church Christ's body, all its members may remain firm in the unity of that body through the enduring bond of love.

We are right to pray that this may be brought about in us through the gift of the one Spirit of the Father and the Son. The holy Trinity, the one true God, is of its nature unity, equality and love, and by one divine activity sanctifies its adopted sons. That is why Scripture says that *God's love has been poured into our hearts by the Holy Spirit he has given us.* The Holy Spirit, who is the one Spirit of the Father and the Son, produces in those to whom he gives the grace of divine adoption the same effect as he produced among those whom the Acts of the Apostles describes as having received the Holy Spirit. We are told that *the company of those who believed were of one heart and soul,* because the one Spirit of the Father and the Son, who with the Father and the Son is one God, had created a single heart and soul in all those who believed.

This is why Saint Paul in his exhortation to the Ephesians says that this spiritual unity in the bond of peace must be carefully preserved. *I, therefore, a prisoner for the Lord,* he writes, *beg you to lead a life worthy of your calling, with all humility and meekness and with patience, bearing with one another in love, eager to maintain the unity of the Spirit in the bond of peace. There is one body and one Spirit.*

God makes the Church itself a sacrifice pleasing in his sight by preserving within it the love which his Holy Spirit has poured out. Thus the grace of that spiritual love is always available to us, enabling us continually to offer ourselves to God as a living sacrifice, holy and pleasing to him for ever. ❧

CHRIST IS THE BOND OF UNITY

Saint Cyril of Alexandria, Bishop

[*From a Commentary on the Gospel of John*]

All who receive the sacred flesh of Christ are united with him as members of his body. This is the teaching of Saint Paul when he speaks of the mystery of our religion *that was hidden from former generations, but has now been revealed to the holy apostles and prophets by the Spirit; namely, that the Gentiles are joint-heirs with the Jews, that they are members of the same body, and that they have a share in the promise made by God in Christ Jesus.*

If, in Christ, all of us, both ourselves and he who is within us by his own flesh, are members of the same body, is it not clear that we are one, both with one another and with Christ? He is the bond that unites us, because he is at once both God and man.

With regard to our unity in the Spirit, we may say, following the same line of thought, that all of us who have received one and the same Spirit, the Holy Spirit, are united intimately, both with one another and with God. Taken separately, we are many, and Christ sends the Spirit, who is both the Father's Spirit and his own, to dwell in each of us. Yet that Spirit, being one and indivisible, gathers together those who are distinct from each other as individuals, and causes them all to be seen as a unity in himself. Just as Christ's sacred flesh has power to make those in whom it is present into one body, so the one, indivisible Spirit of God, dwelling in all, causes all to become one in spirit.

Therefore, Saint Paul appeals to us to *bear with one another charitably, and to spare no effort in securing, by the bonds of peace, the unity that comes from the Spirit. There is but one body and one Spirit, just as there is but one hope held out to us by God's call. There is one*

Lord, one faith, one baptism, one God and Father of all, who is above all, and works through all, and is in all. If the one Spirit dwells in us, the one God and Father of all will be in us, and he, through his Son, will gather together into unity with one another and with himself all who share in the Spirit.

There is also another way of showing that we are made one by sharing in the Holy Spirit. If we have given up our worldly way of life and submitted once for all to the laws of the Spirit, it must surely be obvious to everyone that by repudiating, in a sense, our own life, and taking on the supernatural likeness of the Holy Spirit, who is united to us, our nature is transformed so that we are no longer merely men, but also sons of God, spiritual men, by reason of the share we have received in the divine nature. We are all one, therefore, in the Father and the Son and the Holy Spirit. We are one in mind and holiness, we are one through our communion in the sacred flesh of Christ, and through our sharing in the one Holy Spirit. ❧

CHRIST LIVES IN HIS CHURCH

Saint Leo the Great, Pope

[*From a Sermon*]

My dear brethren, there is no doubt that the Son of God took our human nature into so close a union with himself that one and the same Christ is present, not only in the firstborn of all creation, but in all his saints as well. The head cannot be separated from the members, nor the members from the head. Not in this life, it is true, but only in eternity will God be all in all, yet even now he dwells, whole and undivided, in his temple the Church. Such was his promise to us when he said: *See, I am with you always, even to the end of the world.*

And so all that the Son of God did and taught for the world's reconciliation is not for us simply a matter of past history. Here and now we experience his power at work among us. Born of a virgin mother by the action of the Holy Spirit, Christ keeps his Church spotless and makes her fruitful by the inspiration of the same Spirit. In baptismal regeneration she brings forth children for God beyond all numbering. These are the sons of whom it is written: *They are born not of blood, nor of the desire of the flesh, nor of the will of man, but of God.*

In Christ Abraham's posterity is blessed, because in him the whole world receives the adoption of sons, and in him the patriarch becomes the father of all nations through the birth, not from human stock but by faith, of the descendants that were promised to him. From every nation on earth, without exception, Christ forms a single flock of those he has sanctified, daily fulfilling the promise he once made: *I have other sheep, not of this fold, whom it is also ordained that I shall lead; and there shall be one flock and one shepherd.*

Although it was primarily to Peter that he said: *Feed my sheep,* yet the one Lord guides all pastors in the discharge of their office and leads to rich and fertile pastures all those who come to the rock. There is no counting the sheep who are nourished with his abundant love, and who are prepared to lay down their lives for the sake of the good shepherd who died for them.

But it is not only the martyrs who share in his passion by their glorious courage; the same is true, by faith, of all who are born again in baptism. That is why we are to celebrate the Lord's paschal sacrifice with the unleavened bread of sincerity and truth. The leaven of our former malice is thrown out, and a new creature is filled and inebriated with the Lord himself. For the effect of our sharing in the body and blood of Christ is to change us into what we receive. As we have died with him, and have been buried and raised to life with him, so we bear him within us, both in body and in spirit, in everything we do. ❧

Our Hearts Are Restless

Our Heart Is Restless until It Rests in You

Saint Augustine, Bishop

[*From the Confessions*]

Y*ou are great, Lord, and worthy of our highest praise; your power is great and there is no limit to your wisdom.* Man, a tiny part of your creation, wishes to praise you. Though he bears about him his mortality, the evidence of his sin and the evidence that you *resist the proud*, yet this man, a tiny part of your creation, wishes to praise you. It is you who move man to delight in your praise. For you have made us for yourself, and our heart is restless until it rests in you.

Lord, help me to know and understand which is the soul's first movement, to call upon you for help or to praise you; or if it must first know you before it can call upon you. But if someone does not know you, how can he call upon you? For, not knowing you, he might call upon someone else instead of you. Or must you first be called upon in order to be known? But Scripture says: *Unless they believe in him, how shall they call upon him. And how shall they believe unless someone preaches to them?*

Those who seek the Lord will praise him. Seeking the Lord they will find him, and finding him they will praise him. Lord, let me seek you by calling upon you, and let me call upon you believing in you, for you have been preached to us. Lord, my faith calls upon you, the faith you have given me, the faith you have inspired in me by the incarnation of your Son and through the ministry of your preacher.

How shall I call upon my God, my Lord and my God? For when I call upon him, I am really calling him into myself. Where within me can my God come? How can God who made heaven and earth come into me? Lord my God, is there anything in me that can contain you? Can heaven and earth, which you have made and in which you have made me, contain you? Or is it true that whatever exists contains you since without you nothing would exist?

Since I do indeed exist and yet would not exist unless you were in me, why do I ask you to come to me?

I am not now in hell, yet you are there. For the psalmist says: *If I descend into hell you are there.* Therefore, my God, I would not exist at all, unless you were in me; or rather, I would not exist unless I were in you *from whom and by whom and in whom all things exist.* Yes, Lord, it is so. To what place do I call you to come, since I am in you? Or from what place are you to come to me? Where can I go beyond the bounds of heaven and earth, that my God may come to me, for he has said: *I fill heaven and earth?*

Who will help me to find rest in you? Who will send you into my heart to inebriate it, so that I will forget my evil ways and embrace you, my only good? What are you to me? Have mercy on me, that I may speak. What am I to you that you command me to love you, and grow angry and threaten me with terrible punishment if I do not? Is it then a small sorrow not to love you?

In your mercy, Lord my God, tell me what you are to me. *Say to my soul, I am your salvation.* So speak that I may hear you. The ears of my heart are turned to you, Lord; open them and say to my soul: *I am your salvation.* I will run after your voice and I will lay hold of you. Do not hide your face from me. Let me see your face even if I die, for if I see it not, I shall die of longing. ᔕ

LOVE DESIRES TO SEE GOD

Saint Peter Chrysologus, Bishop

[*From a Sermon*]

When God saw the world falling to ruin because of fear, he immediately acted to call it back to himself with love. He invited it by his grace, preserved it by his love, and embraced it with compassion. When the earth had become hardened in evil, God sent the flood both to punish and to release it. He called Noah to be the father of a new era, urged him with kind words, and showed that he trusted him; he gave him fatherly instruction about the present calamity, and through his grace consoled him with hope for the future. But God did not merely issue commands; rather with Noah sharing the work, he filled the ark with the future seed of the whole world. The sense of loving fellowship thus engendered removed servile fear, and a mutual love could continue to preserve what shared labor had effected.

God called Abraham out of the heathen world, symbolically lengthened his name, and made him the father of all believers. God walked with him on his journeys, protected him in foreign lands, enriched him with earthly possessions, and honored him with victories. He made a covenant with him, saved him from harm, accepted his hospitality, and astonished him by giving him the offspring he had despaired of. Favored with so many graces and drawn by such great sweetness of divine love, Abraham was to learn to love God rather than fear him, and love rather than fear was to inspire his worship.

God comforted Jacob by a dream during his flight, roused him to combat upon his return, and encircled him with a wrestler's embrace to teach him not to be afraid of the author of the conflict, but to love him. God called Moses as a father would, and with fatherly affection invited him to become the liberator of his people.

In all the events we have recalled, the flame of divine love enkindled human hearts and its intoxication overflowed into men's senses. Wounded by love, they longed to look upon God with their bodily eyes. Yet how could our narrow human vision apprehend God, whom the whole world cannot contain? But the law of love is not concerned with what will be, what ought to be, what can be. Love does not reflect; it is unreasonable and knows no moderation. Love refuses to be consoled when its goal proves impossible, despises all hindrances to the attainment of its object. Love destroys the lover if he cannot obtain what he loves; love follows its own promptings, and does not think of right and wrong. Love inflames desire which impels it toward things that are forbidden. But why continue?

It is intolerable for love not to see the object of its longing. That is why whatever reward they merited was nothing to the saints if they could not see the Lord. A love that desires to see God may not have reasonableness on its side, but it is the evidence of filial love. It gave Moses the temerity to say: *If I have found favor in your eyes, show me your face*. It inspired the psalmist to make the same prayer: *Show me your face*. Even the pagans made their images for this purpose: they wanted actually to see what they mistakenly revered. ❧

OUR HEART LONGS FOR GOD

Saint Augustine, Bishop

[*From the Tractates on the First Letter of John*]

We have been promised that *we shall be like him, for we shall see him as he is*. By these words, the tongue has done its best; now we must apply the meditation of the heart. Although they are the words of Saint John, what are they in comparison with the divine reality? And how can we, so greatly inferior to John in merit, add anything of our own? Yet we have received, as John has told us, an anointing by the Holy One which teaches us inwardly more than our tongue can speak. Let us turn to this source of knowledge, and because at present you cannot see, make it your business to desire the divine vision.

The entire life of a good Christian is in fact an exercise of holy desire. You do not yet see what you long for, but the very act of desiring prepares you, so that when he comes you may see and be utterly satisfied.

Suppose you are going to fill some holder or container, and you know you will be given a large amount.

Then you set about stretching your sack or wineskin or whatever it is. Why? Because you know the quantity you will have to put in it and your eyes tell you there is not enough room. By stretching it, therefore, you increase the capacity of the sack, and this is how God deals with us. Simply by making us wait he increases our desire, which in turn enlarges the capacity of our soul, making it able to receive what is to be given to us.

So, my brethren, let us continue to desire, for we shall be filled. Take note of Saint Paul stretching as it were his ability to receive what is to come: *Not that I have already obtained this*, he said, *or am made perfect. Brethren, I do not consider that I have already obtained it.* We might ask him, "If you have not yet obtained it, what are you doing in this life?" *This one thing I do*, answers Paul, *forgetting what lies behind, and stretching forward to what lies ahead, I press on toward the prize to which I am called in the life above.* Not only did Paul say he stretched forward, but he also declared that he pressed on toward a chosen goal. He realized in fact that he was still short of receiving *what no eye has seen, nor ear heard, nor the heart of man conceived.*

Such is our Christian life. By desiring heaven we exercise the powers of our soul. Now this exercise will be effective only to the extent that we free ourselves from desires leading to infatuation with this world. Let me return to the example I have already used, of filling an empty container. God means to fill each of you with what is good; so cast out what is bad! If he wishes to fill you with honey and you are full of sour wine, where is the honey to go? The vessel must be emptied of its contents and then be cleansed. Yes, it must be cleansed even if you have to work hard and scour it. It must be made fit for the new thing, whatever it may be.

We may go on speaking figuratively of honey, gold or wine—but whatever we say we cannot express the reality we are to receive. The name of that reality is God. But who will claim that in that one syllable we utter the full expanse of our heart's desire? Therefore, whatever we say is necessarily less than the full truth. We must extend ourselves toward the measure of Christ so that when he comes he may fill us with his presence. *Then we shall be like him, for we shall see him as he is.*

The Hope of Seeing God

Saint Gregory of Nyssa, Bishop

[*From a Homily*]

The happiness God promises certainly knows no limits. When one has gained such a blessing, what is left to desire? In seeing God one possesses all things. In the language of Scripture, to see is to have. *May you see the good things of Jerusalem* is the same as *May you possess the good things of Jerusalem*. When the prophet says: *May the wicked man be carried off and not see the glory of the Lord*, he means: *May he not share in the glory of the Lord*.

One who has seen God has, in the act of seeing, gained all that is counted good: life without end, everlasting freedom from decay, undying happiness, a kingdom that has no end, lasting joy, true light, a voice to sing pleasingly in the spirit, unapproachable glory, perpetual rejoicing, in a word, the totality of blessing.

Such is the wonderful hope held out by the beatitudes. As we have seen, the condition for seeing God is purity of heart, and now once more my mind is in confusion, as from an attack of giddiness, wondering if purity of heart is something impossible, something beyond the capacity of human nature. If the vision of God is dependent on purity in heart, and if Moses and Paul did not attain this vision—they state that neither they nor anyone else can see God—then the promise of the beatitude spoken by the Word seems to be something impossible of realization.

What do we gain from knowing the means by which God may be seen if we have not the power to see him? It is like saying that one is blessed if one is in heaven because in heaven things are seen that are not seen on earth. If we were told beforehand how to get to heaven, it would be helpful to know that one is blessed if one is in heaven. But as long as the way to heaven is impossible what do we gain by knowing about the happiness of heaven? This only saddens and annoys us when we realize the good things we are deprived of, because it is impossible to get there.

Surely the Lord does not encourage us to do something impossible to human nature because the magnitude of what he commands is beyond the reach of our human strength? The truth is different. He does not command those creatures to whom he has not given wings to become birds, nor those to whom he has assigned a life on land to live in water. If then in the case of all other creatures the command is according to the capacity of those who receive it, and does not oblige them to anything beyond their nature, we shall come to the conclusion that we are not to give up hope of gaining what is promised by the beatitude. John and Paul and Moses, then, and any others like them, did not fail to achieve that sublime happiness that comes from the vision of God: not Paul, who said: *There is stored up for me a crown of righteousness, which the judge who judges justly will give me,* nor John, who leaned on the breast of Jesus, nor Moses, who heard God saying to him, *I know you above all others.*

If it is clear that those who taught that the contemplation of God was beyond their powers are themselves blessed, and if blessedness consists in the vision of God and is granted to the pure in heart, then purity of heart, leading to blessedness, is certainly not among the things that are impossible.

Hence it can be said that those who with Paul teach that the vision of God is beyond our powers are right in what they say, and that the voice of the Lord does not contradict them when he promises that the pure in heart will see God.

Hail, Full of Grace

THE WHOLE WORLD
AWAITS MARY'S REPLY

Saint Bernard, Abbot

[*From a Homily "In Praise of the Virgin Mother"*]

You have heard, O Virgin, that you will conceive and bear a son; you have heard that it will not be by man but by the Holy Spirit. The angel awaits an answer; it is time for him to return to God who sent him. We too are waiting, O Lady, for your word of compassion; the sentence of condemnation weighs heavily upon us.

The price of our salvation is offered to you. We shall be set free at once if you consent. In the eternal Word of God we all came to be, and behold, we die. In your brief response we are to be remade in order to be recalled to life.

Tearful Adam with his sorrowing family begs this of you, O loving Virgin, in their exile from Paradise.

Abraham begs it, David begs it. All the other holy patriarchs, your ancestors, ask it of you, as they dwell in the country of the shadow of death. This is what the whole earth waits for, prostrate at your feet. It is right in doing so, for on your word depends comfort for the wretched, ransom for the captive, freedom for the condemned, indeed, salvation for all the sons of Adam, the whole of your race.

Answer quickly, O Virgin. Reply in haste to the angel, or rather through the angel to the Lord. Answer with a word, receive the Word of God. Speak your own word, conceive the divine Word. Breathe a passing word, embrace the eternal Word.

Why do you delay, why are you afraid? Believe, give praise, and receive. Let humility be bold, let modesty be confident. This is no time for virginal simplicity to forget prudence. In this matter alone, O prudent Virgin, do not fear to be presumptuous. Though modest silence is pleasing, dutiful speech is now more necessary. Open your heart to faith, O blessed Virgin, your lips to praise, your womb to the Creator. See, the desired of all nations is at your door, knocking to enter. If he should pass by because of your delay, in sorrow you would begin to seek him afresh, the One whom your soul loves. Arise, hasten, open. Arise in faith, hasten in devotion, open in praise and thanksgiving. *Behold, the handmaid of the Lord,* she says, *be it done to me according to your word.* ◌

MARY VISITS ELIZABETH

Saint Ambrose, Bishop

[*From a Commentary on Luke*]

When the angel revealed his message to the Virgin Mary he gave her a sign to win her trust. He told her of the motherhood of an old and barren woman to show that God is able to do all that he wills.

When she hears this Mary sets out for the hill country. She does not disbelieve God's words; she feels no uncertainty over the message or doubts about the sign. She goes eager in purpose, dutiful in conscience, hastening for joy.

Filled with God, where would she hasten but to the heights? The Holy Spirit does not proceed by slow, laborious efforts. Quickly, too, the blessings of her coming and the Lord's presence are made clear: *as soon as Elizabeth heard Mary's greeting the child leapt in her womb, and she was filled with the Holy Spirit.*

Notice the contrast and the choice of words. Elizabeth is the first to hear Mary's voice, but John is the first to be aware of grace. She hears with the ears of the body, but he leaps for joy at the meaning of the mystery. She is aware of Mary's presence, but he is aware of the Lord's: a woman aware of a woman's presence, the forerunner aware of the pledge of our salvation. The women speak of the grace they have received while the children are active in secret, unfolding the mystery of love with the help of their mothers, who prophesy by the spirit of their sons.

The child leaps in the womb; the mother is filled with the Holy Spirit, but not before her son. Once the son has been filled with the Holy Spirit, he fills his mother with the same Spirit. John leaps for joy, and the spirit of Mary rejoices in her turn. When John leaps for joy Elizabeth is filled with the Holy Spirit, but we know that though Mary's spirit rejoices she does not need to be filled with the Holy Spirit. Her son, who is beyond our understanding, is active in his mother in a way beyond our understanding. Elizabeth is filled with the Holy Spirit after conceiving John, while Mary is filled with the Holy Spirit before conceiving the Lord. Elizabeth says: *Blessed are you because you have believed.*

You also are blessed because you have heard and believed. A soul that believes both conceives and brings forth the Word of God and acknowledges his works.

Let Mary's soul be in each of you to proclaim the greatness of the Lord. Let her spirit be in each to rejoice in the Lord. Christ has only one mother in the flesh, but we all bring forth Christ in faith. Every soul receives the Word of God if only it keeps chaste, remaining pure and free from sin, its modesty undefiled. The soul that succeeds in this proclaims the greatness of the Lord, just as Mary's soul magnified the Lord and her spirit rejoiced in God her Savior. In another place we read: *Magnify the Lord with me.* The Lord is magnified, not because the human voice can add anything to God but because he is magnified within us. Christ is the image of God, and if the soul does what is right and holy, it magnifies that image of God, in whose likeness it was created and, in magnifying the image of God, the soul has a share in its greatness and is exalted. ❧

THE MAGNIFICAT

Saint Bede the Venerable, Priest

[*From a Commentary on Luke*]

M*ary said: My soul proclaims the greatness of the Lord, my spirit rejoices in God my Savior.* The Lord has exalted me by a gift so great, so unheard of, that language is useless to describe it, and the depths of love in my heart can scarcely grasp it. I offer then all the powers of my soul in praise and thanksgiving. As I contemplate his greatness, which knows no limits, I joyfully surrender my whole life, my senses, my judgments, for my spirit rejoices in the eternal Godhead of that Jesus, that Savior, whom I have conceived in this world of time.

The Almighty has done great things for me, and holy is his name.

Mary looks back to the beginning of her song, where she said: *My soul proclaims the greatness of the Lord.* Only that soul for whom the Lord in his love does great things can proclaim his greatness with fitting praise and encourage those who share her desire and purpose, saying: *Join with me in proclaiming the greatness of the Lord; let us extol his name together.*

Those who know the Lord, yet refuse to proclaim his greatness and sanctify his name to the limit of their power, *will be called least in the kingdom of heaven.* His name is called holy because in the sublimity of his unique power he surpasses every creature and is far removed from all that he has made.

He has come to the help of his servant Israel for he has remembered his promise of mercy.

In a beautiful phrase Mary calls Israel the servant of the Lord. The Lord came to his aid to save him. Israel is an obedient and humble servant, in the words of Hosea: *Israel was a servant, and I loved him.*

Those who refuse to be humble cannot be saved. They cannot say with the prophet: *See, God comes to my aid; the Lord is the helper of my soul.* But *anyone who makes himself humble like a little child is greater in the kingdom of heaven.*

The promise he made to our fathers, to Abraham and his children for ever.

This does not refer to the physical descendants of Abraham, but to his spiritual children. These are his descendants, sprung not from the flesh only, but who, whether circumcised or not, have followed him in faith. Circumcised as he was, Abraham believed, and this was credited to him as an act of righteousness.

The coming of the Savior was promised to Abraham and to his descendants for ever. These are the children of promise, to whom it is said: *If you belong to Christ, then you are descendants of Abraham, heirs in accordance with the promise.* ∾

She Who Believed by Faith, Conceived by Faith

Saint Augustine, Bishop

[*From a Sermon*]

Stretching out his hand over his disciples, the Lord Christ declared: *Here are my mother and my brothers, anyone who does the will of my Father who sent me is my brother and my sister and my mother.* I would urge you to ponder these words. Did the Virgin Mary, who believed by faith and conceived by faith, who was the chosen one from whom our Savior was born among men, who was created by Christ before Christ was created in her—did she not do the will of the Father? Indeed the blessed Mary certainly did the Father's will, and so it was for her a greater thing to have been Christ's disciple than to have been his mother, and she was more blessed in her discipleship than in her motherhood. Hers was the happiness of first bearing in her womb him whom she would obey as her master.

Now listen and see if the words of Scripture do not agree with what I have said. The Lord was passing by and crowds were following him. His miracles gave proof of divine power, and a woman cried out: *Happy is the womb that bore you, blessed is that womb!* But the Lord, not wishing people to seek happiness in a purely physical relationship, replied: *More blessed are those who hear the word of God and keep it.* Mary heard God's word and kept it, and so she is blessed. She kept God's truth in her mind, a nobler thing than carrying his body in her womb. The truth and the body were both Christ: he was kept in Mary's mind insofar as he is truth, he was carried in her womb, in so far as he is man; but what is kept in the mind is of a higher order than what is carried in the womb.

The Virgin Mary is both holy and blessed, and yet the Church is greater than she. Mary is a part of

the Church, a member of the Church, a holy, an eminent—the most eminent—member, but still only a
member of the entire body. The body undoubtedly is
greater than she, one of its members. This body has
the Lord for its head, and head and body together
make up the whole Christ. In other words, our head
is divine—our head is God.

Now, beloved, give me your whole attention, for
you also are members of Christ; you also are the body
of Christ. Consider how you yourselves can be among
those of whom the Lord said: *Here are my mother and
my brothers.* Do you wonder how you can be the
mother of Christ? He himself said: *Whoever hears and
fulfills the will of my Father in heaven is my brother and
my sister and my mother.* As for our being the brothers
and sisters of Christ, we can understand this because
although there is only one inheritance and Christ is
the only Son, his mercy would not allow him to
remain alone. It was his wish that we too should be
heirs of the Father, and coheirs with himself.

Now having said that all of you are brothers of
Christ, shall I not dare to call you his mother? Much
less would I dare to deny his own words. Tell me
how Mary became the mother of Christ, if it was

not by giving birth to the members of Christ? You, to whom I am speaking, are the members of Christ. Of whom were you born? "Of Mother Church," I hear the reply of your hearts. You became sons of this mother at your baptism, you came to birth then as members of Christ. Now you in your turn must draw to the font of baptism as many as you possibly can. You became sons when you were born there yourselves, and now by bringing others to birth in the same way, you have it in your power to become the mothers of Christ. ❦

Mary and the Church

Blessed Isaac of Stella, Abbot

[*From a Sermon*]

The Son of God is the firstborn of many brothers. Although by nature he is the only-begotten, by grace he has joined many to himself and made them one with him. For to those who receive him *he has given the power to become the sons of God.*

He became the Son of man and made many men sons of God, uniting them to himself by his love and power, so that they became as one. In themselves they are many by reason of their human descent, but in him they are one by divine rebirth.

The whole Christ and the unique Christ—the body and the head—are one: one because born of the same God in heaven, and of the same mother on earth. They are many sons, yet one son. Head and members are one son, yet many sons; in the same way, Mary and the Church are one mother, yet more than one mother; one virgin, yet more than one virgin.

Both are mothers, both are virgins. Each conceives of the same Spirit, without concupiscence. Each gives birth to a child of God the Father, without sin. Without any sin, Mary gave birth to Christ the head for the sake of his body. By the forgiveness of every sin, the Church gave birth to the body, for the sake of its head. Each is Christ's mother, but neither gives birth to the whole Christ without the cooperation of the other.

In the inspired Scriptures, what is said in a universal sense of the virgin mother, the Church, is understood in an individual sense of the Virgin Mary, and what is said in a particular sense of the virgin mother Mary is rightly understood in a general sense of the virgin mother, the Church. When either is spoken of, the meaning can be understood of both, almost without qualification.

In a way, every Christian is also believed to be a bride of God's Word, a mother of Christ, his daughter and sister, at once virginal and fruitful. These words are used in a universal sense of the Church, in a special sense of Mary, in a particular sense of the individual Christian. They are used by God's Wisdom in person, the Word of the Father.

This is why Scripture says: *I will dwell in the inheritance of the Lord.* The Lord's inheritance is, in a general sense, the Church; in a special sense, Mary; in an individual sense, the Christian. Christ dwelt for nine months in the tabernacle of Mary's womb. He dwells until the end of the ages in the tabernacle of the Church's faith. He will dwell for ever in the knowledge and love of each faithful soul. ❧

EVE AND MARY

Saint Irenaeus, Bishop

[*From a Treatise "Against Heresies"*]

The Lord, coming into his own creation in visible form, was sustained by his own creation which he himself sustains in being. His obedience on the tree of the cross reversed the disobedience at the tree in Eden; the good news of the truth announced by an angel to Mary, a virgin subject to a husband, undid the evil lie that seduced Eve, a virgin espoused to a husband.

As Eve was seduced by the word of an angel and so fled from God after disobeying his word, Mary in her turn was given the good news by the word of an angel, and bore God in obedience to his word. As Eve was seduced into disobedience to God, so Mary was persuaded into obedience to God; thus the Virgin Mary became the advocate of the virgin Eve.

Christ gathered all things into one, by gathering them into himself. He declared war against our enemy, crushed him who at the beginning had taken us captive in Adam, and trampled on his head, in accordance with God's words to the serpent in Genesis: *I will put enmity between you and the woman, and between your seed and her seed; he shall lie in wait for your head, and you shall lie in wait for his heel.*

The one lying in wait for the serpent's head is the one who was born in the likeness of Adam from the woman, the Virgin. This is the seed spoken of by Paul in the letter to the Galatians: *The law of works was in force until the seed should come to whom the promise was made.* He shows this even more clearly in the same letter when he says: *When the fullness of time had come, God sent his Son, born of a woman.* The enemy would not have been defeated fairly if his vanquisher had not been born of a woman, because it was through a woman that he had gained mastery over man in the beginning, and set himself up as man's adversary.

That is why the Lord proclaims himself the Son of Man, the one who renews in himself that first man from whom the race born of woman was formed; as by a man's defeat our race fell into the bondage of death, so by a man's victory we were to rise again to life. ❧

THE WORD TOOK OUR NATURE
FROM MARY

Saint Athanasius, Bishop

[*From a Letter*]

The Apostle tells us: *The Word took to himself the sons of Abraham, and so had to be like his brothers in all things.* He had then to take a body like ours. This explains the fact of Mary's presence: she is to provide him with a body of his own, to be offered for our sake. Scripture records her giving birth, and says: *She wrapped him in swaddling clothes.* Her breasts, which fed him, were called blessed. Sacrifice was offered because the child was her firstborn. Gabriel used careful and prudent language when he announced his birth. He did not speak of "what will be born *in you*" to avoid the impression that a body would be introduced into her womb from outside; he spoke of "what will be born *from you,*" so that we might know by faith that her child originated within her and from her.

By taking our nature and offering it in sacrifice, the Word was to destroy it completely and then invest it with his own nature, and so prompt the Apostle to say: *This corruptible body must put on incorruption; this mortal body must put on immortality.*

This was not done in outward show only, as some have imagined. This is not so. Our Savior truly became man, and from this has followed the salvation of man as a whole. Our salvation is in no way fictitious, nor does it apply only to the body. The salvation of the whole man, that is, of soul and body, has really been achieved in the Word himself.

What was born of Mary was therefore human by nature, in accordance with the inspired Scriptures, and the body of the Lord was a true body. It was a true body because it was the same as ours. Mary, you see, is our sister, for we are all born from Adam.

The words of Saint John: *The Word was made flesh*, bear the same meaning, as we may see from a similar turn of phrase in Saint Paul: *Christ was made a curse for our sake.* Man's body has acquired something great through its communion and union with the Word. From being mortal it has been made immortal; though it was a living body it has become a spiritual one; though it was made from the earth it has passed through the gates of heaven.

Even when the Word takes a body from Mary, the Trinity remains a Trinity, with neither increase nor decrease. It is for ever perfect. In the Trinity we acknowledge one Godhead, and thus one God, the Father of the Word, is proclaimed in the Church.

Biographical Index of Authors

St. Aelred of Rievaulx (1110-1167) was born in Hexham, England. After working in the court of the King of Scotland, he left to become a Cistercian monk at Rievaulx, Yorkshire, England, where he was eventually named abbot. He was famous for his preaching and wrote many sermons and prayers.

St. Ambrose (c. 340-397) was born in Germany and raised in Rome. He held several important government posts until he was unanimously elected bishop by both Christians and Arians. Forced to accept the nomination, he was baptized and consecrated bishop. In 386, he defied an imperial order to turn churches over to the Arians, and also defeated attempts to restore pagan worship. His eloquent sermons led to St. Augustine's conversion. He is a Doctor of the Church.

St. Asterius of Amasea (died around 410) was born in Pontus in Asia Minor, became a rhetorician, and then was ordained and made bishop of Amasea. He was noted for his preaching, and twenty-one of his sermons are still in existence.

St. Athanasius (c. 297-373) is known as the champion of orthodoxy for his tireless defense of the faith against the Arian heresy. He was born in Alexandria and was elected bishop of that city about 327. As bishop, he was exiled five times by emperors who sided with the Arians. He wrote the famous *On the Incarnation* and numerous other theological works.

St. Augustine (354-430) was born at Thagaste in Northern Africa to a Christian mother and pagan father. As a young man, he joined a heretical sect but converted to Christianity in 387. He was ordained in 391 and made bishop of Hippo in 395. Augustine wrote prolifically on doctrine and Scripture, and is considered the most influential theologian in the history of Christianity. He is a Doctor of the Church.

St. Basil the Great (330-379) was born in Caesarea, Cappadocia, in Asia Minor. He became a hermit in 358 and, after attracting disciples, organized the first monastery in Asia Minor. As archbishop, he helped the poor and sick, and encouraged the clergy to live holy lives. His treatises and other works, including *On the Holy Spirit*, have greatly influenced Christian doctrine. He is a Doctor of the Church.

St. Bede the Venerable (c. 672-735) was born in England and became a monk at a nearby monastery in Wearmouth-Jarrow, where he spent most of his life studying and writing. In addition to his biblical commentaries, he wrote a history of the English Church. He was made a Doctor of the Church in 1899.

St. Bernard of Clairvaux (1190-1153) was born in Burgundy, France, and as a young man, entered Cîteaux, a Cistercian monastery, bringing with him thirty of his relatives and friends. Soon he was sent to establish the monastery of Clairvaux, where he was abbot for thirty-eight years. Mystic, theologian, preacher, and counselor to kings and popes, Bernard was considered the most eloquent and influential man of the twelfth century. Among his many writings are the famous treatise *On Loving God* and his sermons on the Song of Songs. He was declared a Doctor of the Church in 1830.

St. Caesarius of Arles (470-543) was born in Burgundy, France, of a French-Roman family. During the forty years he served as bishop of Arles, he instituted many reforms, brought the Divine Office into the local parishes, founded a convent, and presided over many church councils. Pope St. Symmachus appointed him apostolic delegate to France. He was especially known for his clear sermons, in which he explained practical truths with examples drawn from daily life.

St. Clement I (died around 99) was, according to tradition, baptized by St. Peter. He became pope in 91, and was exiled by the Emperor Trajan but continued preaching to his fellow prisoners in Crimea. Scholars agree that he authored a letter to the Corinthians rebuking them for a split in their church. He died in exile.

St. Cyprian (c. 200-258) was a pagan lawyer when he converted to Christianity in 246. A biblical scholar, he was elected bishop of Carthage in 248, but went into hiding the next year because of a Christian persecution. When he returned, he had to deal with schismatics and a plague that was blamed on Christians. He wrote numerous works on the Bible, the church, prayer, and the requirements for those who had lapsed from their faith but desired to return. He was beheaded during the persecution of Christians by the Emperor Valerian.

St. Cyril of Alexandria (c. 376-444) was born in Alexandria, Egypt, and was made patriarch of that city in 412. He fought against the Nestorian heresy, and wrote treatises that clarified the doctrines of the Trinity and the Incarnation. He was declared a Doctor of the Church in 1882.

St. Fulgentius (468-533) was born of a noble family in Carthage and became a monk when he was twenty-two years old. In 499, he was arrested by an Arian priest and tortured, then released. Appointed bishop of Ruspe in Tunisia in 508, he was banished twice at the instigation of Arian bishops. His treatises defending the orthodox position so influenced the king that he was permitted for a short while to return to his see.

St. Gregory of Nazianzen (c. 329-389) was born in Nazianzus in Cappadocia, and ordained in 362 by his father, who was bishop. When a group of bishops invited him to Constantinople to help restore orthodoxy, his eloquent preaching led many former Arians to convert. He was named archbishop of Constantinople in 380, but resigned shortly afterwards when the validity of his election was questioned. He is known for his great defenses of orthodoxy and the decrees of the Nicene Council.

St. Gregory of Nyssa (c. 330-c. 395) was the brother of St. Basil and was born at Caesarea, Cappadocia. Educated in rhetoric, he became disenchanted by his students and was ordained a priest. He was named bishop of Nyssa, Lower Armenia, in 372, but was imprisoned and exiled by Arians. He wrote many treatises and was considered a great defender of orthodoxy.

St. Hilary of Poitiers (died around 368) was born in Poitiers, Gaul, into a noble family. He was already an older man and married when he converted to Christianity. He was elected bishop of Poitiers around 350, and became immersed in the Arian controversy. He was exiled for several years for his defense of orthodoxy. He wrote numerous treatises, including *On the Trinity*, and was declared a Doctor of the Church in 1851.

St. Irenaeus (c. 125-c. 203) was born in Asia Minor and sent by St. Polycarp as a missionary to Gaul, where he evangelized the area around Lyons. He became bishop of Lyons in 178 after the previous bishop was martyred in a Christian persecution. He strongly opposed the Gnostic heresy, and his five-book treatise against Gnosticism earned him a reputation as a great theologian.

Blessed Isaac of Stella (c. 1100-c. 1169) was born in England and worked for the archbishop of Canterbury before entering Cîteaux, a Cistercian monastery in France, in 1145. He was chosen abbot of Stella, another Cistercian abbey, two years later. Among his sermons are those given to a group of monks during Lent on a solitary island. In 1162, he wrote an epistle on the soul.

St. John Chrysostom (c. 347-407) was born in Antioch, Syria. After his ordination in 386, he became famous for his preaching (Chrysostom means "golden-mouthed"), along with his homilies on the books of the New Testament. He was made Patriarch of Constantinople in 398, and his denunciations of the extravagant lifestyles of the ruling class led to exile, where he eventually died. He was declared a Doctor of the Universal Church at the Council of Chalcedon in 451.

St. Leo the Great (died 461) was born in Rome and elected to the papacy in 440, after serving as deacon under the previous two popes. He delivered a famous series of ninety-six sermons, and clarified the doctrine of the Incarnation at the Council of Chalcedon. After barbarians attacked Rome, he helped to rebuild the city. He was named a Doctor of the Church in 1754.

St. Peter Chrysologus (406-c. 450) was born in Imola, Italy, and was named bishop of Ravenna in 433. His preaching made such an impact on the empress that she enthusiastically supported his building projects. Noted for his homilies (Chrysologus means "golden-worded"), he was named a Doctor of the Church in 1729.